Self-development

A facilitator's guide

David Megginson and Mike Pedler

McGRAW-HILL BOOK COMPANY

London · New York · St Louis · San Francisco · Auckland
Bogotá · Caracas · Hamburg · Lisbon · Madrid · Mexico · Milan
Montreal · New Delhi · Panama · Paris · San Juan · São Paulo
Singapore · Sydney · Tokyo · Toronto

Published by
McGRAW-HILL Book Company Europe
Shoppenhangers Road, Maidenhead,
Berkshire SL6 2QL, England
Telephone 0628 23432
Fax 0628 770224

British Library Cataloguing in Publication Data
Megginson, David
  Self-development : a facilitator's guide
  I. Title II. Pedler, Mike
  658.314

  ISBN 0-07-707460-2

Library of Congress Cataloging-in-Publication Data
Megginson, David,
    Self-development: a facilitator's guide/David Megginson and
  Mike Pedler.
      p.   cm. — (McGraw-Hill training series)
    Includes bibliographical references and index.
    ISBN 0-07-707460-2
    1. Employees—Training of. 2. Self-culture. I. Pedler, Mike.
  II. Title. III. Series.
  HF5549.5.T7M417   1992
  658.3'124—dc20   91-42095
                                                                          CIP

Typeset by Book Ens Limited, Baldock, Herts
Printed and bound in Great Britain by Clays Ltd, St Ives plc

Contents

For Viv, without whom this would not have been written; and to Katherine and Edward, without whom writing would have had much less purpose

For Kath, from whom I get most of my good ideas

Series preface

Training and development are now firmly centre stage in most organizations, if not all. Nothing unusual in that—for some organizations. They have always seen training and development as part of the heart of their businesses—but more and more must see it the same way.

The demographic trends through the nineties will inject into the marketplace severe competition for good people who will need good training. Young people without conventional qualifications, skilled workers in redundant crafts, people out of work, women wishing to return to work—all will require excellent training to fit them to meet the job demands of the 1990s and beyond.

But excellent training does not spring from what we have done well in the past. T&D specialists are in a new ball game. 'Maintenance' training—training to keep up skill levels to do what we have always done—will be less in demand. Rather, organization, work and market change training are now much more important and will remain so for some time. Changing organizations and people is no easy task, requiring special skills and expertise which, sadly, many T&D specialists do not possess.

To work as a 'change' specialist requires us to get centre stage—to the heart of the company's business. This means we have to ask about future goals and strategies and even be involved in their development, at least as far as T&D policies are concerned.

This demands excellent communication skills, political expertise, negotiating ability, diagnostic skills—indeed, all the skills a good internal consultant requires.

The implications for T&D specialists are considerable. It is not enough merely to be skilled in the basics of training, we must also begin to act like business people and to think in business terms and talk the language of business. We must be able to resource training not just from within but by using the vast array of external resources. We must be able to manage our activities as well as any other manager. We must share in the creation and communication of the company's vision. We must never let the goals of the company out of our sight.

In short, we may have to grow and change with the business. It will be hard. We shall not only have to demonstrate relevance but also value for money and achievement of results. We shall be our own boss, as accountable for results as any other line manager, and we shall have to deal with fewer internal resources.

The challenge is on, as many T&D specialists have demonstrated to me over the past few years. We need to be capable of meeting that challenge. This is why McGraw-Hill Book Company Europe have planned and launched this major new training series—to help us meet that challenge.

The series covers all aspects of T&D and provides the knowledge base from which we can develop plans to meet the challenge. They are practical books for the professional person. They are a starting point for planning our journey into the twenty-first century.

Use them well. Don't just read them. Highlight key ideas, thoughts, action pointers or whatever, and have a go at doing something with them. Through experimentation we evolve; through stagnation we die.

I know that all the authors in the McGraw-Hill Training Series would want me to wish you good luck. Have a great journey into the twenty-first century.

ROGER BENNETT
Series Editor

About the series editor

Roger Bennett has over twenty years' experience in training, management education, research and consulting. He has long been involved with trainer training and trainer effectiveness. He has carried out research into trainer effectiveness and conducted workshops, seminars and conferences on the subject around the world. He has written extensively on the subject including the book *Improving Trainer Effectiveness*, Gower. His work has taken him all over the world and has involved directors of companies as well as managers and trainers.

Dr Bennett has worked in engineering, several business schools (including the International Management Centre, where he launched the UK's first masters degree in T&D) and has been a board director of two companies. He is the editor of the *Journal of European Industrial Training* and was series editor of the ITD's *Get In There* workbook and video package for the managers of training departments. He now runs his own business called The Management Development Consultancy.

Preface

In this book we offer a comprehensive framework for self-development. There are, of course, many books about self-development. Indeed, it is well placed to become the training and development orthodoxy of the 1990s. Few of these books, however, focus on the facilitator's role, and none that we have read offers a comprehensive range of arenas that can be addressed in a self-developmental way.

We start (in Chapter 1) by defining the field and building on what has already been written about the nature of self-development. Chapter 2 addresses the crucial issue of why and how developers might develop themselves. We believe that developers who don't develop themselves can't develop those around them. The quality of gracious flexibility—moving with the ebb and flow of others' development, sensing and encouraging an awareness of the wider movements in the lives of individuals, groups and organizations—is enormously helped by a continuing attention to one's own development.

Chapter 3 looks at how developers work with others, and focuses on ways of working with individuals. A threefold classification is offered, which explores how instructing, coaching and mentoring can contribute to self-development.

Chapter 4 also has a threefold structure, and explores the processes and skills involved in enabling self-development in groups. Team building, action-learning sets and self-development groups are the three contexts for development considered here. We also address the core skill of making space.

Chapter 5 takes a wider approach, examining the role of the facilitator in working towards the elusive but rewarding vision of the Learning Company. Up-to-the-minute thinking on this concept is outlined, and activities that might contribute to this vision are offered. Chapter 6 presents a biography of development, enabling developers to place themselves within the history, the present state and the future of development, and suggests resources (books, articles, audio tapes and video-tapes) for exploring one's own development further.

Throughout the book we offer examples, exercises, frameworks and models to encourage people in their own development efforts.

DAVID MEGGINSON & MIKE PEDLER

1 This is self-development

The purpose of this first chapter is to outline the idea of self-development and to begin to define the role of the developer within this idea.

Over the past 10 or 15 years, self-development has moved from being a fringe pursuit to a position in the mainstream of management and business development. There can be few training and development programmes in the 1990s that do not include at least a self-development element in their design and delivery.

This is at a time when the training and development field—in industry, commerce, public services and voluntary organizations—is undergoing a massive expansion. Many more people are choosing, or being asked, to take on the role of developer to help with creating organizations fit for the 'information age'. The changing nature of business and organization demands an unprecedented level of learning throughout working life, and many who take on the role of developer will not necessarily be doing so on a full-time basis. Anyone with responsibility for a task, a process or a piece of work will need to have, or have access to, the skills of the developer in order to get that task done well.

In this book we argue that those who take on the role of developer must first be concerned with their own development. It is through understanding how *I* learn, and what motivates *me*, that I can best put myself in the position of the person trying to tackle something new. We are not saying that everyone learns in the same way or that we all have the same motivations—but that through understanding our own learning processes we can become more aware of other people's.

Chapter 2 deals with the self-development of the developer. It encourages you, the reader, to undertake your own self-development as an essential contribution towards being a developer of others.

Without a commitment to our own self-development, we can fall into the trap of prescribing self-development for others without it being part and parcel of our own professional practice. A short historical excursion will illustrate why this is so important and at the same time begin to define the self-development idea.

Where does self-development come from?

Self-development emerged, or perhaps re-emerged, as an idea in training and development in the 1970s and 1980s as a response to the limitations of the earlier idea of 'systematic training'.

Systematic training was an answer to the skills shortages experienced in industrialized countries in the post-war boom years. When industries and economies tried to respond to the massive demands placed on them, they simply did not have the skilled people to produce the goods. In Britain the 1964 Industrial Training Act set up industry training boards to create an adequate supply of skilled 'manpower' (*sic*), especially in craft and operator grades. Systematic training was just that—the approach was scientific/analytic, based on detailed job descriptions, fol-lowed by even more detailed task, skill and needs analyses. This work study process was carried out by qualified training officers who specified training objectives for 'target populations' that followed standard syllabuses on highly structured training programmes that were thoroughly evaluated. Systematic training was often very successful in cutting down the time needed to bring people to the required skill levels.

However, when applied to supervisory or managerial work in industry or to less definable or 'people-centred' jobs, the systematic approach did not work so well. Faced with complexity, variety and general 'unprogrammability', systematic training can be far too prescriptive. This is because it is narrowly defined in terms of the tutor's views of what is needed in terms of what is within the tutor's competence to deliver. While the programmes were well designed and delivered and the returning participants often evaluated them as 'enjoyable', very little seemed applicable in the messy world of practice.

It is this 'transfer of training' problem, as it became known, that led to a change of focus—to the learner and the learning process rather than the trainer and the training process. Learner-centred designs such as action learning, self-development and self-managed learning, in which the learner's work and life tasks became the primary vehicles for learning and development, began to gain in popularity.

We can map this process as a historical sequence of problems (P) and solutions (S), as shown in Figure 1.1.

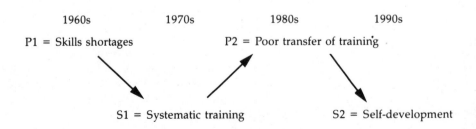

Figure 1.1 *A problem-solution map of training and development*

Self-development can also be seen as a re-emergence of an old idea. In 1938 Dale Carnegie influenced a generation on both sides of the Atlantic with his *How to Win Friends and Influence People*, which urged people to improve themselves and not to rely upon external help, in much the same way that the Victorian Samuel Smiles had done in 1859 with his *Self Help*. In this perspective, the idea of self-development as currently applied to training and development activities reflects a concern to empower the learners, to urge them to take charge and seek out the training and development they need. We are now, again, at a point on the historical wave that weights individual choice and agency over social or organizational definitions of what is needed. This is what makes self-development such a powerful and appropriate idea for now.

Before we move on, it is worth considering whether the current state of the debate overemphasizes self-development at the expense of social and organizational needs. As Figure 1.1 suggests, we are always moving on. Historically it may be that the 1990s was the time in which the emphasis shifted so that we came to balance the powerfully self-asserting individual with new social and organizational definitions of citizenship or membership. This is speculation and will be left to future works; for the moment self-development is in the ascendant and, as we shall see, is regarded as useful in moving organizations, as well as individuals.

What is self-development?

Self-development means that learners take the primary responsibility for choosing what, when and how to learn. This implies the freedom of the individual to choose *not* to develop particular skills, knowledge or career directions at the behest of others. Such freedom, of course, carries with it the responsibility for the consequences of such choices.

Why should people in organizations be given this sort of freedom when they may make choices which are not 'in the interests of the organization'? One answer to this good question is that the world of work is changing so rapidly, with people routinely being called upon to change roles, develop serial careers and swop outdated skills for new ones, that it is increasingly difficult for one person to prescribe for others what they should learn next.

To put it another way, the consequences for the organization of taking one path and getting it wrong are dire, and there is a move towards higher trust employment relations and a realization that the topical claim 'our people are our most valuable asset' needs action as well as fine words.

Second, we no longer use the term 'the organization' with the old taken-for-granted certainty. Systematic training is about meeting organizational needs and requirements. But *who* is the organization and what are its needs? It often turns out that the senior managers define these things. But in these new days of skills shortages, to what extent do senior managers have the power to decide in what direction you or I should develop? Self-development is, in part, an approach which recognizes the increasing power of the 'knowledge worker' who may often have a personal or professional career loyalty first and an organizational loyalty second.

A third answer to the question of why learners should be empowered is that people who choose to develop themselves have much more motivation to learn and succeed than those who are instructed to learn something for the good of 'the organization'. To the extent that the learner chooses directions that benefit the organization—and most of us are highly aware of the context in which we are developing and the trade-offs involved—then you have a self-motivated self-starter who can be relied upon to respond with initiative in a wide variety of circumstances.

It is this self-starting capacity that we are coming to value most highly in people. In Chapter 5, we talk about the 'Learning Company' as a model for the future—an organization that creates learning opportunities for all its members and is also capable of learning and of transforming itself as a collective. Learning Companies cannot operate with people who wait to be taught, who must have permission before they can act, who fear the consequences of taking initiatives. Flexibility and adaptability in both the organization as a whole and in individual members is seen as a critical factor for the future well-being of our enterprises. Self-development as a process offers a way of developing this learning habit:

. . . any effective system for development must increase the learner's capacity and willingness to take control over, and responsibility for, events and particularly for themselves and their own learning.

(Paraphrase from Pedler, Burgoyne and Boydell 1978, p. 1)

Getting started: a self-development primer

We've outlined a few of the principles of self-development, but what does it look like to the self-developer? Here is a primer in seven and a half steps for getting started on self-development:

First, self-development starts with you and with your desire to learn—to learn a job, understand an organization, master a current difficulty, to advance in your career, to be different. Without this desire, self-development cannot start.

NB You don't have to know in precise terms what you want to learn. Most of us don't really know what we need to learn (which is why we so often surrender to 'experts' who will 'diagnose our needs' for us) but you do have to be dissatisfied or feel some discomfort with your present state. Without this you can't start.

Second, you need to understand why you are currently dissatisfied and how you can move forward from this state. This is called self-diagnosis. You always have four choices when you are dissatisfied: to put up with things, to leave, to get others to change or to change yourself. Only if you choose the last option do you need a self-development programme.

There are various ways to get help with self-diagnosis. You can buy a book (some are listed in Chapter 6) that provides a structure and a model of managerial qualities to measure yourself against; you can interview your colleagues, your partner and your customers and ask them how you could improve your service to them; if you're a reflective sort of person, you probably only need to sit and think. You can go to see an expert—a management development person or a chartered psychologist who specializes in psychometric tests—and get an opinion. You can choose a course that offers you some sort of self-diagnostic process as part of the package. There are lots of different ways of going about it and you'll find many more listed in the various recommended books. The main thing is that it is *self*-diagnosis—you are making the decisions and the choices, usually with a little help from your friends.

Third, having diagnosed yourself, you can set yourself some goals for self-development. How would you like the current state to be different? What would the ideal state look like? Write down your goal, in a measurable form if you can, and give yourself a deadline. 'I will get better at asserting myself' is pretty useless (and not very assertive, by the way) as a goal, but 'I will ask Jenny to share the cleaning with me by Friday' is much more like it. If I knew about it, I could ask you how you got on, and we could probably agree (a) how successful you'd been and (b) what else you should try to make yourself more assertive.

There are lots of frameworks for helping you to set goals and most of the self-development books have them. 'Domain mapping' in *Managing Yourself* (Chapter 6) is one example.

Now here is the half step—just when you thought you'd engaged with a nice rational, sequential process. You must take a risk. It might be a little risk—it shouldn't be an enormous risk, unless you're really desperate—but it has to be a risk. Strictly speaking, without risking yourself to some extent—screwing up the courage to approach someone you've been avoiding; deciding to give up a comfortable situation for an unknown, unpredictable, if promising one; asking for something you've never asked for before—there is no development. 'Risk' might be a big word, but to take a chance, a jump into the unknown, to stick your neck out, to put your values on the line, and all those other ways we have of describing this feeling (for that's how you tell when you're at risk—by the feeling in the guts) is a very important part of self-development. Taking these risks or chances, and gaining confidence when they come off, or discovering you're still in one piece when they don't, is perhaps the main component of what makes self-developers 'pro-active' and self-starters.

This is a major paradox for facilitators who, as their name suggests, are there to make things easy. If the facilitator makes things so easy that the risk disappears then so will the development. But how do we know what is the right level of risk? Something I might do without too much thought gives you the willies; what paralyses me, you handle bravely and with no sweat. As with other things, it has to be the learner's decision and, although you—by definition—can never get used to taking risks, you can strengthen your faith in your ability to take risks, to profit from them and survive them.

Fourth (and back to the rational sequence after the jump), armed with some goals, you can set about designing yourself a learning programme and finding the appropriate resources. Obviously, this depends on what you want to learn. In the assertiveness example above, part of the learning programme follows obviously from the goal—a try-out on Jenny— but as preparation you might decide to ask someone or read a book to discover the right form of words in which to put your request. Then you might decide on a rehearsal—with a friend or in front of the mirror or in your head as you go to meet Jenny.

'By March, I will learn to do my accounts on a spreadsheet' is a longer-term goal but the same principles apply. Who can teach you keyboard skills if you don't have them? Could you learn from a book with bits of consultancy from an experienced friend? How much time will you need to practise? Where can you get hold of the machine and the software to practise with? And so on. With a long learning programme you need an overall goal, and also sub-goals to provide staging posts and keep you going.

(We mentioned earlier that 'learning to learn' is the key pay-off from self-development. Part of learning to learn is understanding and internalizing—so that it becomes a part of your professional practice— the process being spelt out here. For example, you'll notice what's involved with developing a learning programme: a goal; some resources, e.g. time for learning; friends or 'learning consultants' to help you; a practice regime; commitment and determination. Knowing this— and being able to do it each time you need it—is a key part of what it means to be able to learn.)

Fifth, as part of this learning-to-learn process, are you noticing how often friends crop up? For most of us learning is a social affair—we need feedback, encouragement and the help of friends to pinpoint our goals, devise our learning programmes and to keep us going. Equally, if we have friends like this, we're probably helping them with their self-development too.

An important part of self-development is the recruiting of other people to help you with your efforts. We call these people 'friends', but they can be all sorts of people—your colleagues, your actual friends, people with particular skills or resources, members of a professional association— and you need to learn to recognize how other people can help you and to build up networks of such people. The reason we call them 'friends' is that we think of them as people who take an interest in our development, people who want us to succeed, and not people who want to put us down, impress us with their knowledge. (Take those who are like this off your 'friends and helpers' file).

You can say with confidence that those who are good at developing themselves have a wide range of contacts and friends with whom they network and stay in touch. Some of the learning methods associated with self-development—especially action learning and self-development groups—make this process of working with a small group of people of central importance. You can find out about these methods from Chapter 4.

Sixth, you have to keep on with your learning programme. 'Stickability' and perseverance—whatever you want to call it. You won't get far without this. 'Genius is 5% inspiration and 95% perspiration', so the saying goes. If spotting your current dissatisfaction is your 5% inspiration, this number SIX will take up much of the rest of your time and energy. Go back to the previous point—self-development has a lot in common with weightwatchers—you're more likely to keep going and succeed if you've got other people with you.

Seventh, and lastly, assess yourself against your goals. How well are you doing? If you set lots of learning sub-goals then these make good points at which to test yourself. It's a bit like being tested at school, but only a bit. Here you set the goals and decide when to test. You interpret the test scores and they're your property. Testing is a healthy process when you're in charge—you need test results to tell you whether you're on track, whether you need to revise future goals and so on.

This seventh point takes you back to the first. Testing yourself leaves you feeling satisfied—in which case you stop learning—or dissatisfied, in which case you carry on, heading for the next target. In the light of this here's an important health warning, which, perhaps, we should have started with:

Important health warning

Self-development can seriously change you and how you think, feel and behave. It should not be undertaken without thought and adequate preparation. For example, your partner, children and colleagues may want you to stay the same. It should not be undertaken lightly by people who have not done any learning for the last decade or two. Self-development can be addictive: people report that learning something 'gives them a buzz' and find they go on to learn more. If this happens on a wide scale it will threaten the fabric of our companies and public service organizations as we know them. You have been warned.

There is much more that could be said about the idea of self-development. If you want to read more about it, you can find a number of sources in Chapter 6. The purpose of this book is not to be a comprehensive guide to what self-development may be, but to focus on developing your practice as a developer. We use the self-development idea to help you think flexibly and creatively about the way in which you act as a developer in the various contexts in which you are working.

The role of the developer

The methods of self-development emphasize learner-centredness and learner control of the process. Some methods of self-development, particularly open and distance learning (which are usually very prescriptive in their approach), are very much D-I-Y, with the developer as a very distant resource. However, many of the methods, such as action learning, give the developer a role that is less concerned with instructing and transmitting information and more concerned with facilitating learners' understanding and helping them to make meaning out of what is going on around them.

However, as we point out in this book, the self-development approach can be used by developers even in settings that require an instructional role. To take a simple example: if you are running an induction programme for new people, you can either tell them what the firm does or you can devise a way of helping them find out—perhaps by having them interview some people from different departments. From the developer's standpoint, self-development for others is about seeking to maximize learner choice and freedom in the learning setting. More ideas on how to do this are found at the end of Chapter 4 in a section called 'Making space: core skill for self-development'.

The developer's role in self-development is to encourage the learner to take primary responsibility for setting personal goals for learning, deciding when and how to learn, when to stop, and how to value what has been learned. The learner wants to be encouraged to do this but is also scared of the responsibility and will often, on the basis of previous experience, try to persuade the developer to be a 'teacher' and tell and explain and give the 'right answers'. When the developer resists this seduction and asks questions instead of giving answers the learner may well become puzzled and, perhaps, frustrated. One of the skills in being a developer in this setting is promoting just enough puzzlement to help the learner enquire further but not so much that it leads to complete frustration. This is not an easy balance to find.

Many self-development designs use tasks as learning vehicles. Instead of working on case studies or exercises, learners work on actual work or life tasks and then reflect on their efforts and learn from them. The developer's role here is to encourage learners to set some goals for action and learning, and to think about the consequences of taking action, and also to encourage them to act in order to create the material for learning. The learners having acted, the developer can then help them observe and reflect on what happened and on what can be learned from what happened. What have they learned about this task? What have they learned about what their strengths are . . . and what they need to get better at? What have they observed about their own preferences and style compared with those of their colleagues? How will they act differently next time? What do they need to learn next? And so on. Work and learning are not separated, as on the training course, but brought together as a continuous whole.

The role of the developer, then, can be seen as helping the learner with the various stages of the learning cycle, as shown in Figure 1.2.

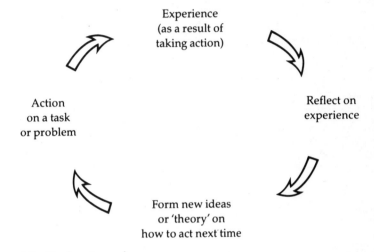

Figure 1.2 *The learning cycle*

As we shall see, in Chapter 4 especially, the developer may not do all these things personally; it is another tenet of self-development that some of the best people to help us with our journey round the learning cycle are our fellow learners. Action-learning sets and self-development groups sometimes take this principle to the logical extreme of eliminating the developer as a separate role altogether, as members pick up these skills and exercise them. At the moment, this tends to happen only in relatively few cases. Most learners, either operating alone or in a small group setting, prefer to have someone with the special responsibility of facilitating learning. As we develop our learning skills we may find this less necessary.

The main task of the developer is to help the learner understand the learning process itself—as, for example, in the diagram above, that learning and action relate together in this way. This can help learners 'learn how to learn', in that they begin to recognize what to do in order to act and learn in unfamiliar situations. The ability to learn how to learn is a key component of self-starters and, in a changing world, is perhaps the best insurance against the inevitable redundancy of our existing stock of knowledge and skills.

The ability to learn how to learn is the real pay-off from the self-development process. Why bother to learn about, say, budgeting or a new technical skill in a self-developmental way when I can be easily instructed to 'operate by numbers'? *Because*, only when you set out to learn because you want to, and in a self-responsible way, can you become aware of the actual processes involved in learning. Internalize these processes, make them part of your practice and, like riding a bicycle, you'll never forget them. That is the key role of the developer, not just to get this or that skill developed, but to help people to acquire that learning capability.

Empowering people to act and learn

To sum up the developer's task in self-development, it is to **empower people to learn from acting and to act on the basis of learning**.

We deal with people, however, in a number of settings, and these settings have a major influence on how we act as developers. In this book we use a simple definition of the developer's field of work and show it as covering four main settings (see Figure 1.3).

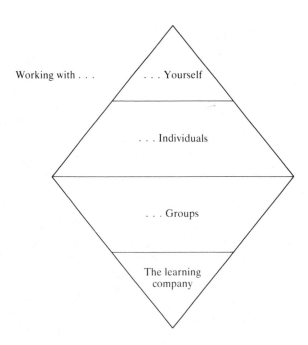

Figure 1.3 Developer's diamond field

This is the developer's diamond field, which appears as a motif at various points in this book. Many of us probably work most with the second and third areas—with individuals and groups—and these settings cover the most ground in the diagram above. We also include working with yourself, as an important precondition for effective work with others, and working with the organization as a whole, which is a newish focus for us and perhaps for many developers.

(Where we use the term 'company' in this context, we refer not to a particular legal form of organization nor to post a bias towards the private sector, but intend the more general sense of 'a company of people' who are 'companions' in an enterprise together, public or private, voluntary or commercial. In this area, the developer's job is perhaps to ensure that we are in 'good company'.)

The diamond field in Figure 1.3 also serves as an overview of this book. There are six chapters—this introductory one, a final 'resources and contacts' chapter and the four in between. Chapter 2 is mainly concerned with working with yourself—acting on your own self-development. As we've said already, we see this as an essential first step and foundation for working with others in the self-development way. Chapter 3 focuses on working with individuals, Chapter 4 on groups and Chapter 3 on what it means to work with the whole company of people in a given enterprise (see Figure 1.4).

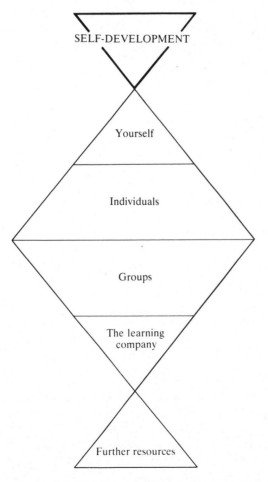

Figure 1.4 *The diamond field overview of this book*

Activity 1.1   *Draw your own diamond field*

Before we move on, stop and think about who you work with. We suggested above that most of us spend most of our time with the middle two areas—individuals and groups. Is this true of your work pattern? Perhaps you spend most of your time with groups, do a small amount of mentoring and counselling with individuals, devote, say, 10 days a year to your own self-development, but don't feel that you work with the organization as a whole in any meaningful way at all. If so, your diamond field of work would look like Figure 1.5.

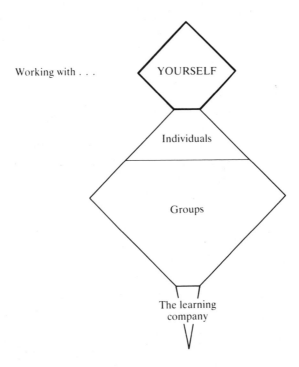

Working with . . .

Figure 1.5   *A personal diamond field of work*

Take a few moments to think about your field of work as a developer. Do you work in all four areas? What proportion of your time is spent in each? Before moving on, draw your own diamond to illustrate your work pattern. Don't worry if your picture isn't in fact a diamond shape—it almost certainly won't be. The point is to get a visual and spatial picture of what the balance of your work looks like. Perhaps we should put 'diamond' in inverted commas. Draw your own work pattern in the space on the opposite page.

Now ask yourself a few questions about your 'diamond'.

1 How do you feel about the overall pattern?
2 Is the pattern determined by 'organizational requirements' or your own preferences?
3 Would you like to change the shape of your diamond?
4 If so, what changes would you like to make?
5 What opportunities exist in your work setting to develop the areas you'd like to move into?

You might like to discuss the answers to these questions with your colleagues. Many developers who are concerned with their own development as well as that of other people feel the need to discuss the question of their work focus and balance from time to time. One way of doing this is to start or join a self-development group with other developers to spend time on these and other professional and personal issues. In Chapter 2 you will find an illustration of this sort of group, and Chapter 6 contains sources if you are interested enough to pursue this further.

Developer or trainer?

Throughout this book we use the term 'developer' instead of 'trainer' for two main reasons. The first of these stems from the historical argument outlined above—that 'training' and 'trainer' are words that are associated in our minds with the systematic training approach, whereas 'developer' with its facilitative rather than teaching overtones is more appropriate for the self-development age. However, we wouldn't want to make too much of this; a rose by any other name would smell as sweet and many 'trainers' engage in facilitation and self-development. It depends how important you think words and their implications are.

The second reason is more solid, we think. We are entering an age when training and development—or perhaps 'human resources' management in general (although we don't like this term)—are attaining a maturity which sees them not only employed as strategic tools by senior managers but also, in a few cases, influencing the strategic thinking process. In some companies, the focus of training and development activities is widening from the traditional one of providing the organization with an adequate supply of skilled people. In times of rapid change when survival and success depend on the company's ability to flex and respond rapidly to customer and other stakeholder demands, training and development activities are used increasingly to help 'change the culture'—'the way we do things around here'. We might flinch sometimes from the cavalier way in which this rich and complex notion of culture is assumed to be so easily manipulable, but there is no doubt that where such culture-change efforts take place the focus for training and development activities is a *collective* rather than an individual one.

Chapter 5 deals with this new focus for the trainer or developer under the heading of the Learning Company—which is the formulation we prefer. Leaving aside arguments as to whether you can really change the culture or not, the important point is that the developer is being asked to think about the organization as a whole. We are being asked to extend our skills so that we can design and intervene at the level of the whole and not just with groups and individuals as many developers have been used to doing. This is a big journey, which many of us are just beginning. It's hard to think in terms of the whole, to keep the whole in mind when we act, as we must, on an individual basis within a small area, influencing only a few colleagues at a time. But this is the challenge of the Learning Company for the developer—to help everybody who makes up this company to act locally while being mindful of the whole.

We think this is the current great challenge for developers, and with this focus the term 'developer' does seem much more appropriate than trainer. To develop means to grow as a whole being, organism or entity; to take that next step; to seek for the next appropriate form to fit our own aspirations and the opportunities presented to us.

The skills of the developer

Skills are learned qualities that belong to the individual. They enable us to do things more quickly and effectively than people who do not possess them. In the case of the developer they take a long time to develop because these are skills with one's self, with other people, with groups and with organizations. These skills are at a premium as we move into the 'information age' where quick fixes and structural alterations alone are of limited value and where new technology eliminates some hard-won skills but creates an urgent demand for new ones.

Once learned, skills can be deeply satisfying to their owner. The practice of apparently mundane skills such as writing in an italic hand or sweeping a yard can bring value and pleasure to the writer/sweeper and to those who are the recipients of the service—as long as we are exercising these skills freely and from a sense of choice. Skilled action displays control and confidence and few things are as healing and 'grounding' as the practice of well-honed skills. This is where many of us maintain ourselves in good order, recover from outrageous fortune and find our purpose and identity.

All skills can be practised at various levels. We can be absolute beginners or artists and still experience the joys and frustrations of competence and incompetence. The true 'master' knows what she doesn't know and, though she may appear supremely competent to others less skilled, knows how far she falls short of where she aims. This is as true for developers as for musicians, painters or pastry cooks. Another plus for the word 'developer' is that it implies that we are still in the process of becoming. We still have a way to go in developing our skills and ourselves and it is this awareness of our 'incompetence'—of what we have yet to learn—as well as what we know we can do, that makes us valuable as helpers and examples to other learners.

For the purpose of doing a little diagnosis on your own areas of competence and incompetence at the developer's craft, we can sketch out four levels of ascending skill:

1 **The learner**—who is learning the rules, procedures and standard ways of doing things. We try hard at this level to do the right thing, to copy elders and betters, and spend most of our time practising. We use exercises as if we were following a recipe and are terrified by the thought of giving a ten-minute input or writing on the flip-chart in front of a group.

2 **The competent worker**—who can operate to the norms and conventions of the developer's trade and can do the job in an acceptable way. At this level we can do most jobs in accordance with current standards. Here we can enjoy giving inputs, be more flexible about the way we run exercises and manage group discussions with aplomb.

3 **The craftsperson**—who is well beyond competence and able to apply skills in new and complex situations. Here, as well as doing the job competently, we are designing our own exercises to fit the requirements of the situation; we attend work meetings and bring the developer's skills and perspective to bear even though we are not in a 'teaching situation'. At this level we have developed certain aspects of ourselves to make a distinctive contribution to the work—so, for example, one person excels at counselling distressed people, another writes with style and verve, yet another uses humour in a very effective way to give feedback.

4 The artist—who is a craftsperson operating with wider awareness in diverse and unfamiliar conditions yet with a clear sense of purpose and mission. For an artist, how things are done is as important as what is done. All artists contribute to the particular needs of the time and place as well as serving a higher purpose. Thinking of developers as artists may be a less familiar idea than thinking of painters or musicians in this way although, if developing is an increasingly important social art, then this is an important aspiration for the trade. As artists, we developers create things of distinctive value that may have lasting relevance. Of particular importance are the values from which we operate and the purpose we are serving. What is the purpose of development? What is the end of development? What are the processes by which development takes place? Who benefits? Who loses? What is the next step in the development of this social art? These are some of the questions likely to exercise the developer as artist.

The purpose of creating these distinctions is not to set up the Institute of Development Practitioners with four grades of membership. In our view, that sort of institutionalization can spell the death of the living process we are trying to describe. However, one of the things that professional bodies exist for is to create and monitor a set of ethical practices and standards for members. As the craft of developing comes into its time, we see a need to establish some standards and ethics of practice. The job of the developer is to work with the living processes involved in themselves, in other people, in groups and in companies. We are not the originators of others' living, human processes and we do not determine their purposes and ultimate direction. However, we can facilitate these processes and influence their direction now. In doing this work we join a high calling and we need the personal and professional rigour to match.

A good part of achieving this is to press on with our own continuing professional and personal development. In fact, this is the best guarantee in the long run, for it is one of the marks of learning that we come to look back on things we used to do and shudder. No professional body, however well run, can change this truth. It is the pain and the glory of learning that it reveals to us both our previous woeful and wilful ignorance, and the knowledge that it is through such folly that we come to be where we are today.

So, where are you today? Have a look at the chart in Figure 1.6. Across the top we have put in the four levels of skill and down the side are listed some of the settings you might find yourself in as a developer. To do this we have borrowed from a model you haven't met yet, of three 'modes' or roles for the developer—instructor, coach and mentor. To find out what these mean in our terms you will have to refer forward to Chapter 3 where we introduce this model as applied to working with individuals, and to Chapter 4 where we use the parallel terms 'direct', 'guide' and 'enable' for working with groups. Perhaps at this stage you might want to guess at the definitions, which we hope have enough face validity to enable you to do this.

Work through the chart putting 'N' (for Now) under one of the four headings for each of the eight settings down the side. For example, if you haven't given much time to thinking about your own development and perhaps suspect that you don't know much about how to do this, you would put 'N' under the Learner column.

Looking at the profile of your skills under these eight settings, you should have something that approximates to the diamond field of work you drew earlier. This profile differentiates more with regard to working with individuals and groups and also places you on a development continuum from Learner to Artist on each of the eight settings.

How do you feel about your current profile? Again, you could discuss this with colleagues. It probably reflects the opportunities you've had and the preferences you've expressed in your work to date. Can you trace your career biography in this chart? Here is where you started . . . that part was acquired first in such and such a place . . . and so on.

When you think you have a fix on where you are now, go back to the chart and go through it again, putting a 'D' (for Desired) against the eight settings for where you'd like to be. You can have the 'D' in the same box as the 'N' if you're satisfied with your current skill level. You wouldn't normally have any 'Ds' to the left of your 'Ns'—unless you actively wanted to give up on or abandon a skill.

What does the chart look like now? It should give you a picture of where the gaps are between where you are now and where you'd like to be. If you have lots of 'Ds' to the right of your 'Ns', then you are clearly intending to develop a number of fronts. Perhaps you are early on in your career as a developer or perhaps you have high aspirations? If you are in the position of having a lot of gaps between where you want to be and where you are now, you will have to choose some priorities for your own development. This is perhaps harder for most of us earlier on in a career, where there is lots of potential and possibilities, than later when we are more formed and our sense of purpose and direction has become clearer. If you want to press forward on lots of fronts, you must spread your effort and look for opportunities across this wide range. Or perhaps you want to specialize and focus on just one development direction next?

Whatever you decide to do, it will probably help to discuss it with other people and perhaps to enshrine your decision in a personal development plan (see Chapter 2).

Having got this far with thinking about your own development to date and forming some idea of where you want to go, it is time to move on to Chapter 2, which is concerned with working with yourself.

	Learner	Competent worker	Craftsperson	Artist
1 *Myself*				
2 *Individual (Instructor)*				
3 *Individual (Coach)*				
4 *Individual (Mentor)*				
5 *Group (Direct)*				
6 *Group (Guide)*				
7 *Group (Enable)*				
8 *The whole company*				

Figure 1.6 *Personal skills profile*

In this chapter we have introduced the idea of self-development and outlined the role of the developer in this process. This helped to explain why the book was written and who it is written for. We believe that there is an increasing demand for people with a developer's skills to work with individuals and organizations to help them meet the challenges of the future.

We introduced the outline of the book, which follows the four settings for development of self, other person, group and whole company. Finally, we looked at the skill levels of the developer and invited you to diagnose yourself by skill level and by work setting. This can be the basis for a personal development plan for yourself.

Reference

Pedler, M., J. G. Burgoyne and T. H. Boydell (1988) *Applying Self-development in Organizations*, Prentice-Hall, Hemel Hempstead.

2 Developing as developers

Who develops the developer?

The old Latin tag, *quis custodiet custodies?* (who guards the guardians?), can be usefully applied to all professions. When it comes to teachers, trainers and developers, life and work can all too easily become development for others. One of our key points is that developers have to look first at developing themselves. How can you promote development in others, if you can't manage it for yourself?

Figure 2.1 is the model we use to highlight some of the areas for developing ourselves.

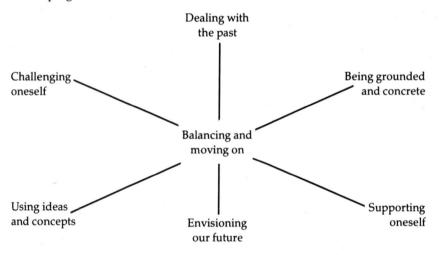

Figure 2.1   Areas for development

This model has three dimensions—past and future; challenging and supporting; abstract and concrete—together with the core notion of balancing and moving on. We can nurture ourselves as developers by taking care of these aspects of our lives. This chapter offers ideas and activities for working in each of the seven areas.

Developing through your past and your future

Most developers have a lot of experience writing CVs—curriculum vitae—which are little potted life histories, usually work-related. It's common to find this a frustrating business—did you ever write one yet to which you could say 'Now—that's really me!'? Usually we emerge from these things as strange two-dimensional creatures, the sort you'd avoid at parties if you had the chance.

Dealing with the past

Knowing who you are and how you came to be this way is vital for developers. Understanding the pattern of our own development—what we inherited, what we learned on the way and what we intend to be in the future—is a fundamental question of our being. We need this awareness to work with others in the process of becoming.

Inheritance is the first major factor in who we are and what we can be. 'One's body, hair and skin are gifts from one's parents, one is not at liberty to do harm to them', said Confucius in presenting a view of self-development that emphasizes the wider context of our development. What other gifts were you given?

Activity 2.1 *My inherited gifts*

'This is a list of gifts I inherited and which I have some responsibility for realizing in my work and life.' (list at least seven)

How aware are you of your inheritance? Did you manage seven or seventeen? We are all richly endowed with gifts and much of our learning is concerned with bringing these potentials to fruition. If you couldn't name at least seven—either because you don't see yourself as 'gifted' or because you think you're primarily self-made—then perhaps you should think harder about this and try out this activity with other people.

Although it is difficult to distinguish learning from inheritance—and pointless in any holistic sense—it is useful to recognize what you have learned and how that learning was achieved. One of the tools we use in development is 'biography work' and one of our favourite activities is given next.

Activity 2.2   Key development events

1 Think of three occasions in your life when you really changed. Changed, that is, in the sense of being different after the event in some qualitative way. The 'event' can be instantaneous, when the world changed in a flash; or it can cover a longish period, such as a first pregnancy. A development event can be major, and literally life-changing, or less dramatic but nevertheless leaving you, in some aspect, a different person.

Think of three events and jot them down in the left-hand column of the chart below.

	Events	*Feelings*	*Outcomes*
1			
2			
3			

2 Now think about how you felt at the time for each of these three events—before, during and after. Jot some feelings against each of the three events you have listed.

3 Now, what is the quality in you today which you trace back to that event—what ability, feeling, attitude, understanding? Write this down for each event in the Outcomes column.

In this way we can trace the origin of some of our enduring qualities and attitudes—things we have learned from experience. Obviously, there are far more than three things you have learned, and if this were a biography group we would be spending more time and unearthing more learnings from your life history. This sort of activity can give you an awareness of what you've learned and the strength with which you hold that quality. Such learnings can be almost as hard to change, to unlearn, as some of your inherited characteristics. It is a salutary lesson for us developers to recognize how fixed we are in some respects. It teaches us to respect others' boundaries and fixed points.

Some of the things we have learned will have been gained painfully. You may have listed such feelings against your events. When we learn, we redeem those painful events by learning from them, and this is the worthy work that developers can do for people. That's why you may have recorded strongly mixed feelings against some of your events— sorrow and joy, anger and calm, and so on. One thing to note is that while you were learning you had some very powerful feelings. Most of us were probably taught that learning is a largely cognitive process—taking place in the head, as it were—but we know that feelings play a very large part in learning and developers need to be able to work with these as well as with reasoning processes.

Some things which have happened to us have been so painful that we haven't managed to redeem them through learning. Some things that happened in early life, or which were devastating in later life, may be so deep and so 'defended' that we never manage to learn from them. These we carry around with us as so much baggage. However, it is especially in relation to this baggage that the old saying 'It's never too late . . .' holds true. A psychoanalytic perspective would see development as concerned with uncovering the unconscious or deeply repressed past and learning to live with yourself and to love what you are.

Dealing with the past means an acceptance of this baggage that all of us carry and which we may learn from literally at any time. We have to learn *both* to carry it, *and* to remain open to the possibility of transformation.

It is important to take stock from time to time as part of knowing who we are and as preparation for moving on. Reviewing life history is to be involved in a re-reading and re-writing of who we are, as one of the delights of self-development is the creative process of constructing new meanings to enrich our lives. Before moving on to the future, here is an activity to help you take stock of your life so far.

Activity 2.3   Me : Current status report

List up to ten things under each heading that you have achieved or been satisfied by in your life so far:

1 Family, friends, relationships

2 Wealth and possessions

3 Career, expertise, professional development

4 Health, personal development and learning

5 Status, influence with others

6 Artistic, cultural, spiritual

What do you think of your lists? How do they make you feel? What does your partner, friend or group think of them?

Which three of the six areas are the most satisfying to you:

1

2

3

With this stock-take we leave the past and move to the future.

Envisioning the future The second factor in who we are and what we become is our future image of ourselves and our will to achieve this. As with the past we can

constantly revise our image of our possibl[...]
inventive and daring about these futures th[...]

We cannot know the future, so there is little[...]
can, however, use imagination to envision v[...]
selves. We can but dream. Dreams may not b[...]
underestimate the power of our thoughts and[...]
thinking about the future is to make a start. Tl[...]
in the future is a very important first step to b[...]

We've mentioned CVs before. Activity 2.4 invit[...]ou to try writing about yourself in the future.

Activity 2.4   Picturing my future

Choose one of the following two activities and spend some time composing a picture of yourself from the given perspective:

- Write your own obituary as you would like it to appear in the news-paper of your choice. When you have finished, read what you have written. What impression does the obituary give? What sort of a person was this? What did they achieve? What was she or he remembered for? What did they leave behind?
- Sit comfortably where you will not be interrupted. Close your eyes and imagine a perfect day at some time in the future. Go over it in some detail. Start with getting up in the morning. Where are you? What is the weather like? What are you doing? Who is with you? What do you do next? How are you feeling? What are the others doing now? Continue right through lunch, the afternoon, evening and finally to going to sleep.

After doing one or both of these activities you will begin to get some-thing of a picture of what is left to do, of your, as yet, unrealized ambitions. We hope this has started to illuminate the future for you. There are many other activities for envisioning the future and you will find some sources listed in Chapter 6, Stream C. Once again this sort of activity gains much from being done with other people, and especially perhaps with a group of like-minded others.

Part of your future vision can be the establishment of goals in the various important areas of your life. Goal and target setting is a dodgy business at times, but thinking through what these might be is as important as any action plan. Even if you don't believe in the value of rational planning or at least are a confirmed sceptic like us, this is useful thinking-through activity.

Activity 2.5   My ambitions for the future

Below are repeated the six areas of life for which you have already listed your achievements and satisfactions. Now go through them again, this time listing your *future* goals.

1 Family, friends, relationships

2 Wealth and possessions

3 Career, expertise, professional development

4 Health, personal development and learning

5 Status, influence with others

6 Artistic, cultural, spiritual

constantly revise our image of our possible future. We can be more inventive and daring about these futures than we think we can.

We cannot know the future, so there is little place here for analysis. We can, however, use imagination to envision various possibilities for ourselves. We can but dream. Dreams may not be reality, but it is easy to underestimate the power of our thoughts and visions. Wondering and thinking about the future is to make a start. The way we see ourselves in the future is a very important first step to bringing it about.

We've mentioned CVs before. Activity 2.4 invites you to try writing about yourself in the future.

Activity 2.4   Picturing my future

Choose one of the following two activities and spend some time composing a picture of yourself from the given perspective:

- Write your own obituary as you would like it to appear in the newspaper of your choice. When you have finished, read what you have written. What impression does the obituary give? What sort of a person was this? What did they achieve? What was she or he remembered for? What did they leave behind?
- Sit comfortably where you will not be interrupted. Close your eyes and imagine a perfect day at some time in the future. Go over it in some detail. Start with getting up in the morning. Where are you? What is the weather like? What are you doing? Who is with you? What do you do next? How are you feeling? What are the others doing now? Continue right through lunch, the afternoon, evening and finally to going to sleep.

After doing one or both of these activities you will begin to get something of a picture of what is left to do, of your, as yet, unrealized ambitions. We hope this has started to illuminate the future for you. There are many other activities for envisioning the future and you will find some sources listed in Chapter 6, Stream C. Once again this sort of activity gains much from being done with other people, and especially perhaps with a group of like-minded others.

Part of your future vision can be the establishment of goals in the various important areas of your life. Goal and target setting is a dodgy business at times, but thinking through what these might be is as important as any action plan. Even if you don't believe in the value of rational planning or at least are a confirmed sceptic like us, this is useful thinking-through activity.

Activity 2.5   My ambitions for the future

Below are repeated the six areas of life for which you have already listed your achievements and satisfactions. Now go through them again, this time listing your *future* goals.

1 Family, friends, relationships

2 Wealth and possessions

3 Career, expertise, professional development

4 Health, personal development and learning

5 Status, influence with others

6 Artistic, cultural, spiritual

What do you think of your lists? How do they make you feel? What does your partner or friend think of them?

Now write down which three of the six areas are the most motivating, that is, where you most want to achieve, in rank order:

1

2

3

Abstract and concrete notions

Being grounded and concrete

In the various traditions of Japanese martial arts, warriors learn to remain rooted to the ground, however hard anyone tries to budge them. In bioenergetics, the trainer notices how the learners stand, sit and walk. Do they place themselves firmly and squarely on the earth? Within both frameworks there is an explicit link between firm standing and being grounded as persons—see Stream C2.2 of Chapter 6.

To gain the virtues of firmness and resolution we need to be grounded and concrete. There are a number of aspects of ourselves which can get in the way of this 'groundedness'. The questionnaire below asks you in which ways you sabotage yourself.

Activity 2.6   Being grounded

Here are five ways of not being grounded. For each time rank yourself on a scale of 0 to 10. If it doesn't apply ever, at all, score 0; if it always applies, is highly characteristic of you, score 10.

- *Intellectualizing*:   'I like playing with ideas'
  'I prefer to see patterns than get things done'
  'I believe it's essential to have a theoretical model before one can act'

Not at all   0   1   2   3   4   5   6   7   8   9   10   Very true
true of me   of me

- *Fantasizing*:   'I can always take comfort in dreams'
  'I imagine the things I might have said and done after the event'
  'I daydream about being different, but somehow it doesn't happen'

Not at all   0   1   2   3   4   5   6   7   8   9   10   Very true
true of me   of me

• *Downheartedness*:   'Life is unfair and I have a bad deal'
'Perhaps I could get away from this situation'
'There's nothing I can do to change things'

Not at all   0   1   2   3   4   5   6   7   8   9   10   Very true
true of me   of me

• *Indecisiveness*:   'I have so many options, I don't know which to choose'
'I can see both sides of every argument'
'With any course of action there are so many unforeseen consequences'

Not at all   0   1   2   3   4   5   6   7   8   9   10   Very true
true of me   of me

• *Stuckness*:   'This is the way I am; I've always been like this'
'I've been doing the same things now for a long time'
'I'm the kind of person who can't . . .'

Not at all   0   1   2   3   4   5   6   7   8   9   10   Very true
true of me   of me

Most of us fall prey to some of these at times. Some of them are very enjoyable and also very useful—in the short term. Fantasizing, for example, can help us learn from events, to observe ourselves and imagine alternatives. It's only when these things become habitual and chronic that they begin seriously to undermine us.

Depending on how self-aware, self-critical and honest you are, you should perhaps think about any scores higher than, say, 3. If you have some of these, ask yourself: 'Am I in danger of being undermined by this tendency? Does it affect my groundedness in an adverse way?'

When you've thought about this, you need to discuss the scores with someone who knows you well and whom you trust. Do you need to take action with regard to any of these, or are they within the bounds of what is normal and acceptable for you?

If you do decide that you want to take action to increase your groundedness and reduce some of these undermining factors, here are several suggested activities for working on each of the five conditions.

Intellectualizing   Whilst we acknowledge the value of thinking things through and being clear, it is very easy to get off the ground and up into the air when theorizing, clarifying, labelling, modelling and developing intellectual frameworks to explain things when all the time there is some pressing and specific work to do NOW. Are you subject to the charms of paralysis by analysis?

If you want to work on this area try the following:

Activity 2.7 *Separating knowing and inferring*

• Write down your thoughts about some current and unresolved issue in your life—a problem at work, a relationship with a child or friend, etc. You can write in notes, in prose, in a list or a mind-map/string bag (see Figure 2.2, p. 34), whatever suits you, but write at some length—at least half a page of A4.

- Review your material and separate *facts* from *assumptions*. You might need some help with this as it isn't always easy to see what our own assumptions are. List these in two columns so you can see how much of what you write falls into each.
- Having got the feel of the distinction, try to practise it by using only *facts* in the next suitable conversation or situation. See how that feels and what benefits and losses accrue.

Fantasizing Earlier in this chapter we talked about a positive way of dealing with the future. Here we are talking not about the constructive, short-term use of fantasizing but about the chronic addiction that is a substitute for reality. As the poet Goethe said:

Whatever you can do or dream you can do : begin it.
Boldness has genius and power and magic in it.
Begin it now!

Here is an activity for dreamers:

Activity 2.8   Transforming dreams

- Take some brief notes of a dream—your next one, a current one or a recurring one.
- Analyse your notes into *feasible* and *unfeasible* components and list them in two columns.
- Against each of the unfeasible components write 'I acknowledge that this dream has no part in my current life and will not shape my actions in the future'. It is important to write this and then to read through the unfeasible dreams again. This may lead you to change the categorization.
- For each of the feasible components, try turning it into a SMART goal statement which is:

  —Specific
  —Measurable
  —Action-oriented
  —Realistic
  —Timely

For example, a dream with a component that shows you being sur-rounded by members of your family could be converted into a goal which said 'By the end of the month I will invite all my family and friends to the housewarming I've not quite had yet'.

Downheartedness There is a very simple activity for those of us tempted overmuch by despair. When we are downhearted, we tend to criticize ourselves for being like that and then perhaps to get angry for criticizing ourselves and so on, in a circular trap. This is an activity for those of us who are fed up with being downhearted. Being downhearted or despairing at times is part of our lot and not to be so at certain times would be psychopathic. But, sometimes we do a lot of it . . . or it goes on too long . . .

Activity 2.9   *Uplifting yourself*

- Write down all your favourite downhearted feelings like the ones given in the questionnaire, e.g. 'I've never had any lucky breaks'. Make a list and keep going until you've written down everything you're feeling.
- Now transform your statements by adding to your phrase or sentence. You can often put simple words like 'so far today' or 'since I last saw Diane' which completely change the original. So, for example, 'I've never had any lucky breaks *at work in the last month*' puts a quite different perspective on the original. Transform all your statements in this way.
- Now read through your statements and decide on two things you could do to uplift yourself. You might find that just putting your downhearted feelings on paper and then into a wider context helps you to think differently about them. Or you might decide it's time you saw Diane again, or to be ill for the day and off work. Do something uplifting.

Indecisiveness   'I used to be indecisive, but now I'm not sure' is an old joke that shows how this affliction, like downheartedness, feeds on itself. On the other hand, as the saying goes, 'the world rewards action', and decisiveness is just as catching as its shadow side. Some people are so decisive it gives you a pain. But how can we, with full regard for the possible consequences, act thoughtfully? Here's a case study that shows one way.

Jane's job

Jane had just completed a taxing full-time development programme in consultancy skills. She was unclear about what to do next. She knew she wanted a rest, so she didn't apply for jobs or seek work as an independent consultant. After two months she became restless but still felt unable to decide. Also, her money was running out.

Jane decided to try a *rational decision-making model*, listing all the options she could think of and identifying the pros and cons of each. This helped a bit. She elaborated one option (academic work) but was still left with two balanced directions—employment as an internal consultant or self-employment. Neither seemed wholly right.

She then went inside herself and attended to her feelings. She could not see full-time paid employment offering her what she wanted in terms of lifestyle—she would feel fettered by regular hours and organizational demands. On the other hand, she felt unsure and unworthy about being an external consultant. 'Have I the track record? How will I handle the business side?' she asked.

With the help of a 'speaking partner' she did some work on valuing her own ability to shape her world, so as to feel less threatened by the constraints of employment. She also recognized that much of her feeling of incompetence stemmed, not from a real appraisal of her experience and current abilities, but from old messages from her parents and primary school headteacher. She resolved to let these messages go.

Both options now appeared more attractive, but she was still unclear about which to go for. She then determined to do something—anything—that week, and see what happened. She heard some friends talking about the possibility of consulting and said 'Oh, I've decided to go freelance. Is there a role for me?' To her surprise, they said 'Yes'.

It sounds simple, written like this, but actually, at the time, she hadn't decided to go freelance, she had just tried it on for size. Two years later, Jane is operating successfully as an independent consultant. As it happens, the partnership with her two friends did not work out but she had made a decision, anyway. Every now and then she has a strong desire to go back into paid employment—which she might do some day. Having made one difficult decision, there seems no reason why she shouldn't make another when the time comes . . . the world rewards action.

Rational decision-making approaches can be useful at times but, with difficult or momentous choices, there is always a muddling-through element. The lesson from Jane's story appears to be that following hunches or intuition, taking action without planning, has a very important place too. Action—in whatever direction—always creates information, and information often reduces uncertainty. Try it. You can always change your mind later.

'Stuckness' Garrison Keillor quotes the motto of his home town, Lake Wobegone, as *sumus quod sumus*—we are what we are. While, on the one hand, this might indicate a self-acceptance that is the very essence of groundedness, in the case of many of the citizens of Lake Wobegone it signifies something else too—'I'm stuck', 'I can't/won't change', 'I'm just that kind of person'. If you won't change, then fine, that's your privilege. If you want to change but feel stuck, try the next activity.

Activity 2.10   Becoming unstuck

Letting go of the past.   This is a lifetime task, but here are some simple exercises for this time. Do at least one of these or one of your own design:

- Give to Oxfam all the clothes you haven't worn in the last two years.
- Throw out all the files, notes, manuals you haven't used in the last five years.
- Ring the people you've promised something to but haven't delivered yet and say 'It doesn't look likely in the near future, but I do feel good about you and if circumstances change I'll be in touch. Meanwhile, I'm getting rid of a lot of baggage to get my world clear.'

Loving and valuing yourself.   You have to start from here. Paradoxically, it's hard to change if you don't accept yourself for what you are. This is a difficult thing for many of us to do but if we, as developers, can't make an effort, how are we to support and work with others on their self-development? You can try this affirmation as part of the process of creating positive self-esteem—**'I am loving and capable'**.

Generally speaking, we can move forwards only from a position of being supported—especially by ourselves. We do not move from being under attack. Co-counsellors emphasize: 'In every situation I have always done the very best I can' (given what I know, how I have developed, etc.) So blame—particularly self-blame—for failings is irrelevant to moving forwards.

Accepting the possibility of change.   Just to remind yourself, fill in the chart below as fully as possible:

Things I can do now but couldn't 5 years ago	*Things I could do 5 years ago but not 10*	*Things I could do 10 years ago but not 15*

Enough said?

Affirming your goal.   We're always punishing ourselves with goals and deadlines that don't give us much joy even when we manage to meet them. Try to put your goal in terms that affirm and reward you. An affirmation:

- is a statement in the present tense about having met the goal
- specifies how you might experience the outcome
- includes feelings and elaborates your experience

So, for example, don't say 'I'm going to finish this chapter by 30 September' (even if it kills me); say, 'I am really enjoying posting the finished draft to my co-author on 30 September, and confidently expecting his warm congratulations for the quality and timeliness of the work'.

Try this approach on one of the areas in which you experience yourself as being stuck. When you've written it, stick it up somewhere where you'll see it frequently. Read it out loud at least once a day and as often as you like. Tell somebody important about it, and above all . . . tell yourself.

To summarize this section. Being grounded and concrete is about acquiring and sustaining the firmness and balance needed for the developmental struggle. We've outlined five of the main dragons in this region. Intellectualizing and fantasizing keep us up in the air, and to bring ourselves down we must be specific and concrete. 'Stuckness' and being downhearted undermine us and we have to dig ourselves out. Being indecisive means that, although we are on the ground, we lack a firm stance. We can acquire this by moving purposefully.

Using ideas and concepts

Fields of knowledge are like string bags. There is no single, right way to enter them—which is a pleasing thought for all those who were put off chemistry for life by the table of elements, or French by the pages of grammar. We can pick up a new area of knowledge anywhere, at any knot in the bag, and find it is connected to all the other bits.

This is a liberating concept for self-developers because it means you can start learning something new without being sure you're starting in 'the right place'. Our philosophy is that the right place is the one that seems appropriate to you now; and if it's right because you decided to do something today and this is it . . . well, so be it. If you can learn French without starting with the grammar—go to it.

In self-development, starting with our own ideas is very important. Our ideas either gain power by being pursued, explored, enthused over and used, or we realize, as a result of these activities, how daft they are. The important first step is to give yourself power as a learner: we can all think; we can all have ideas; we can all develop our ideas.

We are not saying that your ideas are better than other people's, but that, in a way, you can only have your own ideas. When you read or hear something that sounds interesting, and think about it, make sense of it, start using it, tentatively at first, then you are making something your own—wherever it came from in the first place. You have no way of knowing whether your understanding is what X meant when she wrote the words that started off your idea. You should perhaps acknowledge your source as part of the good tradition of honouring those who go before—but it was you who chose it, fitted it into your string bag and now take responsibility for propagating it.

Many people have learned from their schooling that 'knowledge' means the reproduced ideas of others. We have often not been rewarded for producing our own ideas and theories—quite the contrary. So, many of us in later life say, 'I'm not an original thinker, I can't . . .' and usually we are doing one or more of the following:

• putting ourselves down and not allowing ourselves to have ideas
• not giving ourselves time to be creative and play with theories
• not sharing tentative, fanciful thoughts with others

If these ring a bell try this:

Activity 2.11   Thinking

Select an area of your life and work where you're bogged down in detail and can't see the wood for the trees.

- Define the issue. Write down—in the very middle of a blank sheet of nice paper—what it is you want to resolve, understand more about or come to terms with. Write it down now; it doesn't matter if you don't 'get it right' at this stage!
- Now, in a free-floating or brainstorming sort of way, start writing down issues, factors, ideas, possibilities that seem to be connected to your first statement, on the other parts of the page. Draw lines attaching your first statement to the others. If you see that some of the other statements link up with each other, then draw lines between those too.
- Show your string bag to a friend. Ask him or her to help you—not to get it 'right', whatever that means, but to make it richer. Ask the friend for ideas that might fit. Discuss these and add any which you can see are useful. Remember you are the authority on what fits into your string bag.
- Look at your bag. What would be a good point at which to pick up the issue now? If you pick it up there, what other issues or notions are connected most closely? Now try to build a statement around these links.

As an example, we reproduce part of a bag that one of us made to help with the ideas used in 'being grounded and concrete', elsewhere in this chapter:

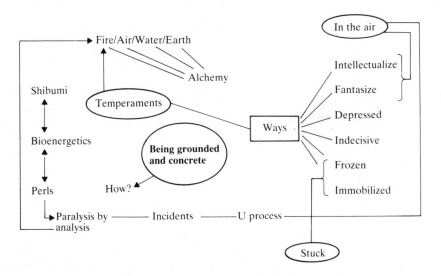

Figure 2.2   A 'string' bag

Does that help? Once again we're not saying that the above is 'right' in any other way than that it helped us to write this chapter and, we hope, provides you with something you can use to develop yourself.

What we want to emphasize in this section is that each of us has the capacity to think, to make sense and to have good ideas. The process of producing something like the above goes like this:

- ask 'Why?'
- play with ideas
- give yourself some time
- allow yourself not to get it 'right'
- involve friends
- make use of the ideas of others (with their permission) and
- always knit your own string bag

Challenging and supporting yourself

Take up the challenge! Taking critical feedback is hard work for most of us. Assertiveness trainers talk of 'fogging'—of being like a fog, not resisting anything that's given but not letting it stick either.

We use the model shown in Figure 2.3 to help us receive feedback constructively, filtering out that which is meant to harm us from that which we can use to develop ourselves. How we receive it is as important as what is given—if I don't receive it properly, then the best-constructed feedback will have only negative effects:

Here is an activity to test this out:

Activity 2.12   Learning from mistakes

- List a number of recent mistakes you've made. Against each one note what part you played. Who else was involved?
- Pick one from your list. Now *assume* that you were entirely at fault— that the mistake was 'entirely *my* responsibility'. Even if you played a relatively minor part in your recollection, work out a way of describing it so that it stems entirely from some action or inaction of yours. OK?

So, for example, a deadline was missed in producing a report to a major client. One of your staff failed to provide the information in time. Someone else sent the report second class mail. Royal Mail took four days to deliver, etc. When we review mistakes in this way, it's always easy to allocate blame, with most of it directed elsewhere.

Let's see how you were responsible. With your staff member—had you made it clear how important that information was? Had you made the

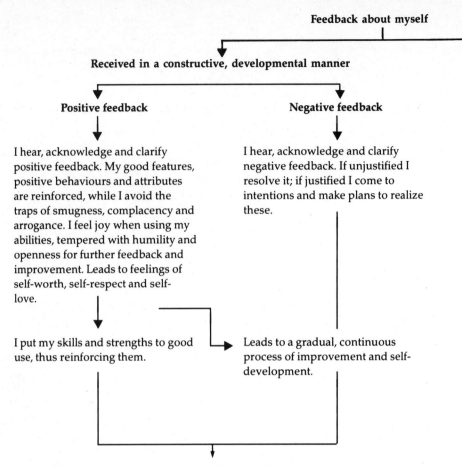

Feedback about myself

Received in a constructive, developmental manner

Positive feedback

Negative feedback

I hear, acknowledge and clarify positive feedback. My good features, positive behaviours and attributes are reinforced, while I avoid the traps of smugness, complacency and arrogance. I feel joy when using my abilities, tempered with humility and openness for further feedback and improvement. Leads to feelings of self-worth, self-respect and self-love.

I hear, acknowledge and clarify negative feedback. If unjustified I resolve it; if justified I come to intentions and make plans to realize these.

I put my skills and strengths to good use, thus reinforcing them.

Leads to a gradual, continuous process of improvement and self-development.

Feelings of self-respect, self-worth, self-love enable me to respect, value and love others. This and the resultant ability to manage myself lead to mutually enhancing and developmental relationships with other people in my family, friends, community, organization, etc. Positive spiral of two-way feedback.

Source: Reproduced from Pedler, M.J. and T.H. Boydell *Managing Yourself*, Fontana 1985, pp. 74–75 with permission.

Figure 2.3   *Receiving feedback*

Received in a non-constructive, regressive manner

Positive feedback

I become proud, smug, complacent. Alternatively, I don't in fact hear positive feedback, or I deny it, or play it down, with overriding bad or negative self-image and feelings about myself.

I continue to avoid other opportunities for change, improvement and development, preferring to remain stuck with an unrealistic sense of my own brilliance, and/or resting on my laurels rather than facing up to new challenges.

Negative feedback

My negative feelings about myself are reinforced; and/or I feel threatened and insecure and therefore ignore or deny the feedback, often attacking or running away from its source.

I continue to refuse to look at my negative aspects in order to improve. Subconsciously I am probably dimly aware of these, and therefore I grow to dislike, despise or hate myself. Often this is accompanied by an urge for self-destruction, and an inability to find, recognize and use the strengths that I do in fact possess.

Certainly no development. Indeed, my combination of smugness and self-hatred, coupled with my consequent inability to manage myself, probably lead to regression and even damage or destruction to myself, family, relationships, organization or community.

deadline clear? Had you reorganized that person's workload so that they could do the job in time? With the person who did the posting—was he briefed properly? Did he have the power to pay for express mail or courier? Are you sure that none of your past actions influenced what happened? With Royal Mail—was the address fully correct? Had you really ensured enough leeway for time in the mail?

While at one level it may be appropriate or just to ascribe some responsibility to others, from a learning angle there's a lot of mileage in the process described above. Not to blame yourself, but to confront yourself with your own actions or inactions in the situation. We are not suggesting that you should take responsibility for everything all the time—our world is too complicated, too interactional for that to make any sense, as well as it being a recipe for demolishing your self-esteem on a permanent basis—but that the regular exercise of confronting ourselves and our own actions is an essential skill and habit for self-developers. The skill lies in being able to challenge yourself appropriately but still maintain the confidence to go forward in action and in development, and at some time—inevitably—to make the next mistake. Activity 4.13 on page 102 can be used as a development of this one.

There are, of course, other ways in which you can challenge yourself or, rather, put yourself in challenging situations. Being part of an action-learning set (see Chapter 4) is one way that provides us with 'comrades in adversity'—friends prepared to act as 'enemies'—and it can also give that precious glimpse of how others see us going about and acting in the world. However, no one can provide you with the raw material for a challenge unless you are prepared to receive it—unless you are able to challenge yourself.

Enough of challenge: by now you must be in need of support.

Support yourself   Being a developer can be an isolating business. We work intensively with people, often at a deeply personal level. When we share of ourselves it is to support and encourage others. Or it should be. So even at the end of a week where we feel we haven't had a moment alone, we can feel drained and isolated. At such times we are prey to self-doubt and weakness. Confidence and energy may vanish with frightening suddenness.

As we said earlier, the developers' first responsibility is to themselves. This applies very strongly to supporting yourself. If you don't take care of yourself, who will? This is often best done by enlisting the help of others, but you start by making the commitment to yourself. When you need it, from whom do you get that support, that taking in of substance, so that you can continue giving it out?

Before moving on, take time to think about where you get your support from.

Activity 2.13   Your support network

Who . . .   *Names*

. . . is around when I need them?

. . . makes me feel competent and valued?

. . . can I share bad news with?

. . . cheers me up?

. . . can I share good news with?

. . . 'gives it to me straight'?

. . . is prepared to sit and listen to me?

Look at your list of names. Have you any obvious gaps? Are you putting too much on one or two people? How could you add to your support network?

We asked a group of management development consultants, who met together as a men's self-development group, where they got their support. They offered a range of supports although, characteristically for men:

- several felt they did not have enough support people
- several talked of really close, old friends, who in practice they had not seen for a number of years!

All five members included the self-development group in their list, remarking on the importance of this 'safe place' to which they could return. As people who usually work alone they find the self-development group invaluable. Figure 2.4 gives a brief account of how their group works—the design principles.

- *Joining: the initiator doesn't invite everyone*
  The initiator asked two people to join him, and the three acquired four more.

  Why? To share ownership and create new familiar people for all.

- *A commitment to six meetings*
  Six meetings were agreed at the start, followed by a review. One person had dropped out by then.

  Why? Early meetings can be difficult; a medium-term commitment can pull us through and encourage experiment and risk.

- *Sharing time*
  While we can manage time in any way we agree, a basic principle is to start each meeting with bids for time. Time is person-based, not issue-based.

  Why? A minimal structure that gives direction and legitimizes helping interventions.

Figure 2.4   *Design principles of a men's self-development group*

- *No trainer*
  At first the idea of special events with an invited trainer was discussed, but at times we felt as if we had five trainers helping the focal person; at times, the last person we'd have wanted present was a trainer.

  Why? We believe in people's ability to help themselves—let's practise what we preach.

- *Different ways of being together*
  In three years of regular meetings we've had occasional residential events involving walking, risking our necks rock climbing, painting, singing and writing poems together.

  Why? Shifting the medium encourages the sharing of different competencies and different terrors; it gives us all new experiences and encourages us to see ourselves as continually developing.

- *Open agenda*
  People wrote different things in their diaries to denote the meeting dates: one wrote 'men's group', another 'consultants' group', another simply 'the group'. In three years we've discussed consulting, marketing our services, money, home/work balance, gender and sexuality, even death.

  Why? Purposes and needs can emerge slowly. Don't limit yourselves at the start—allow for growth.

- *The competitive dragon*
  All groups have dragons, and ours was feelings of competition. Six of us were independents working the same area. In the early days we showed off about clients or held back information; eventually we confronted this.

  Why? Competition was a block we had to surmount in order to build trust.

- *Confidentiality*
  We don't speak, even to our partners, about the specific content of other people's issues.

  Why? Security.

Figure 2.4   *(cont'd)*

The self-development group is just one way of creating a source of support for ourselves. This group evolved its principles to create a climate for effective work. Having such a group perhaps ensures that members do not make unethical use of client groups for personal support and therapy.

Some people have found that a pair relationship such as co-counselling or 'speaking partners' is the right vehicle for providing their support. Obviously, there are many others who might be willing and able to help us, including friends and family members, but it often helps to have someone or some group from outside your immediate circle. Whatever the support arrangements, similar principles to those sketched out in Figure 2.4 might be applicable.

People we know use many other sources of support ranging through exercise, meditation, massage, batik-making, gardening and other hobbies and leisure activities.

One of the very useful self-skills for developers is the ability to give yourself treats. If you take it unto yourself to tackle tough tasks, then you need to give yourself some treats too. These can range from long, hot baths or weekends at health farms to allocating 30 days a year to your own development—to do the new or keep the old alive. One developer we know promises herself 24 weekday walking days a year.

What are your treats?

Are you treating yourself well?

The balancing act of self-development

Balancing and moving on

There are times when we all get stuck, periods when life and work lose their sparkle. We may feel bored, listless, without energy. Or it might be feelings of despair or self-doubt that assail you?

The onset of crisis—for such moments *are* crises, major or minor—can be difficult for developers. After all, we're around to help others with their development. How can we carry on when we are feeling like this?

Such crises signal a phase in the development cycle. We've come to the end of something, perhaps something that has served us well and is now less satisfying, no longer acceptable. We don't want to leave our familiar past, our hard-won skills, our companions behind; yet we must. We have to move on, but we feel lost. What does the future hold? What direction should we take? We can't see it.

The silver lining is this: as development is our business, if we can begin to understand the process in and around ourselves, we will emerge better equipped and with an enhanced ability to help ourselves and others. Indeed, it takes only a moment's reflection to realize that we would not be able to do our jobs without this experience of development—the endings, new directions and crises, the self-questioning and loss of direction that are involved from time to time.

One way of thinking about crisis is to use the idea that we have become temporarily unbalanced. Here are a few ways in which we can get out of balance:

- the loss of a friend or close relationship
- working too hard
- having a run of bad luck
- being overconcerned or obsessed about money
- drifting, without clear goals, unfocused
- being preoccupied with self and losing interest in others
- being so concerned with what's happening outside that we pay no attention to ourselves, and lose touch with ourselves.

For developers, these last two are particularly important.

Good mental health requires a balance of inner and outer. (See Figure 2.5 on p. 43.) Too much inner can lead to morbid introspection; too much outer to blind self-sacrifice. As developers we need to work with these polarities in ourselves as well as with our clients.

Here's a balance check for you:

Activity 2.14   Balancing life scales

Here are some pairs of words with spaces in between. Put an 'N' between each pair of words to show where you think you are Now and an 'I' to show where you would Ideally like to be. Because there are six spaces you have to lean to one side or the other.

Add your own pairs of words for other aspects of your life.

Work							Home
Inner							Outer
Adults							Children
Home							Leisure/hobbies
Fun							Seriousness
Time for others							Time for me
Doing							Being
Women							Men
Relationships							Career

Imbalances are not necessarily bad. Einstein probably spent more time than you or I would want to, working out mathematical equations, yet he seems to have had a satisfying life and emerged as a highly developed human being as well as a scientific superstar. The question is: how do you feel about your life balances?

Figure 2.5   *A balanced state of mental health*

Perfect balance is unusual—that's one reason we put six spaces in Activity 2.14. We might attain this momentarily, but not for most of the time. For example, on Home and Work, you might now be bringing up young children or caring for someone at home. This is bound to create an imbalance but perhaps that feels right for you? Or you might be putting a lot into work just now, and that's what you want to do. Both of these imbalances are temporary in that they belong to this phase of your life, although they may go on for years.

There are a great number of these dimensions in the lives of us all and they exist in a sort of tension. There is nothing fixed about the way we currently divide up our time and attention, but the way we make that division will depend very much on our purpose in life and that of the people close to us. To simplify the matter a little, Figure 2.6 shows three major areas that exist in most people's lives.

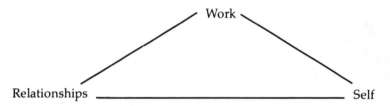

Figure 2.6   *Major life dimensions*

Activity 2.15   *Triangulating your life*

- Looking at the triangle in Figure 2.6, position yourself with regard to your current life balance. You can do this by putting a cross inside (or, indeed, outside) the triangle to illustrate where you are in relation to these three broad aspects of life. If you are a young parent with a newborn child, you might see your life as being nearly all about relationships; if you are newly retired you might experience having lots of space for your Self.
- When you have positioned yourself, you can draw lines to the three aspects to show how near to them you are, or how far away from them.
- How does your life look now compared with how you'd like to be? Do some clear imbalances emerge? Now, place a second cross inside the triangle to show where you would ideally like to be.

What direction(s) have you moved in? Away from what . . . and towards what? Trace the movement you will have to make to move from where you are now to where you'd like to be. Can you see what needs to be done?

Moving from analysis to action, here is an activity to help you keep your balance.

Activity 2.16   *Keeping your balance*

- First identify three imbalances from your 'balancing life scales' chart (Activity 2.14) or from the general survey of Work *vs.* Self *vs.* Relationships.
- Write them down in this form—'I see an imbalance between . . . . and . . . .'.
- Against each imbalance write the name(s) of any other people involved.
- Talk to the various people concerned—one at a time. Check out your perceptions of the situation and get their views.
- If there is a real difference of opinion, then negotiate around what is reasonable. Here are three headings you could use for yourself and for the other person to help create a constructive negotiation:
  —What you do now that I would like you to continue doing
  —What you do now that I would like you to stop doing
  —What you do *not* do now that I would like you to start doing

Chapter 2 has been about giving time to you—the developer—as the most important and first step in developing others. Now it's time to move on to Chapter 3, which begins the sequence of three chapters concerned with helping other people to develop—as individuals, in groups and in companies.

Reference

Pedler, M. J. and T. H. Boydell (1985) *Managing Yourself*, pp. 74–5, Fontana.

3 Working with individuals

In this chapter we consider the role of the facilitator working one-to-one with others

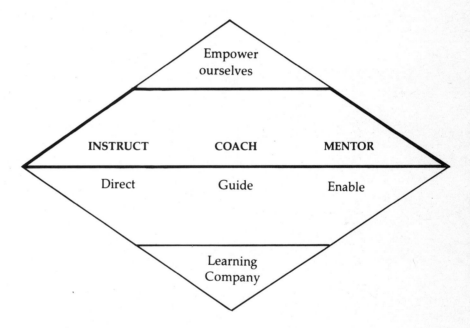

Figure 3.1 *Helping individuals*

Whether you are a trainer, a consultant or a line manager, when working one-to-one you are likely to have a big impact on people.

In this chapter we outline ways of using your skills so as to enable learners to make their own sense of what you say—even when you are being relatively directive.

Another point about working with individuals is that, as the word suggests, individuals are *un-divided*. So even if your help is connected to quite a small part of their life or work, be open to the possibility that it could have wide implications for the learner. For example, someone being taught keyboard skills may be thinking, 'Will this trap me into certain routine kinds of jobs?' or 'Will this training mean they'll be expecting me to work full-time, and what effect will this have on my family?' It is important to address these questions if they arise.

Instructor, coach, mentor

As Figure 3.1 suggests, we propose three alternative ways of being a one-to-one facilitator—*instructor*, *coach* and *mentor*. Activity 3.1 enables you to explore the extent to which you use these three approches.

Activity 3.1   *Exploring my one-to-one helping style*

Step 1   Complete the questionnaire by circling one of the numbers (1–6) for each question. You may find it easy to focus on how you are helping one individual, or you may want to look more generally at your overall approach.

1 Before telling people about a job I want them to do, I work out stage by stage what's involved in it:

   Never   1   2   3   4   5   6   Often

2 I actively seek out opportunities for them to develop themselves through doing new things at work:

   Never   1   2   3   4   5   6   Often

3 I listen to their ideas, and help them fit these into their broad plans for work and life:

   Never   1   2   3   4   5   6   Often

4 When I have something I want them to do, I give people very clear instructions:

   Never   1   2   3   4   5   6   Often

5 I help them to plan how they can meet challenges at work:

   Never   1   2   3   4   5   6   Often

6 I ask them questions that help them to think through why they want to do things:

   Never   1   2   3   4   5   6   Often

7 I check that they have got their instructions accurately:

   Never   1   2   3   4   5   6   Often

8 I am prepared to let people try out new skills even if there's a risk they may not do the job well:

   Never   1   2   3   4   5   6   Often

9 I am interested in what they do outside work, and how this fits or conflicts with work activities:

   Never   1   2   3   4   5   6   Often

10 I check up on things I've asked them to do, and let them know how they did:

   Never   1   2   3   4   5   6   Often

11 I encourage learners to review how they perform, and to plan how to improve:

Never   1   2   3   4   5   6   Often

12 I sit down with them and help them to think about where they are going in their career:

Never   1   2   3   4   5   6   Often

Step 2   To interpret your scores, total up the numbers you have circled for each of the three columns below:

Instructor	*Coach*	*Mentor*
Q1	Q2	Q3
Q4	Q5	Q6
Q7	Q8	Q9
Q10	Q11	Q12
Total ____	Total ____	Total ____

The higher your score in any column, the more of that approach you tend to use.

Step 3   You may wish to get a friend to assess your emphasis on these three areas—you might ask them to complete the questionnaire indicating how they see you. You may also like to compare your scores against norms for 47 managers and trainers who have completed the same questionnaire. Their average scores on the three scales were:

Instructor = 15.04   Coach = 14.11   Mentor = 13.63

Step 4   Now refer to Table 3.1 and the accompanying text, which outlines what the three styles involve.

Step 5   There is no right or wrong answer as to what the scores 'should' be for every case. You can find out what your staff think of your style by asking them. Some basic questions to ask yourself would be:

• Do I agree with the results of the questionnaire? If not, what mix of styles do I use?
• Does this mix of styles achieve my objectives for helping this person?
• Does my style meet the needs of my learner
  —in the short term?
  —in the longer term?
• How could I amend my style to meet these needs more effectively?

What differentiates the three styles? We outline the main differences in Table 3.1 on the following page and then illustrate with examples.

Table 3.1 *Three ways of helping managers to learn*

Dimension	Instructor	Coach	Mentor
Focus of helping	Task	Results of job	Individual person developing through life
Timespan	A day or two	A month to a year	A career or lifetime
Approach to helping	Show and tell; give supervised practice	Explore problem together, and set up an opportunity for learner to try out new skills	Act as a friend willing to play the part of an adversary; listen; question to enlarge conscious-ness; listen some more
Associated activities	Analysing task; clear instruction; supervising practice; immediate feedback on errors; consolidation	Jointly identifying the problem; creating oppor-tunities for development; developmental reviewing	Linking work with other parts of one's life; clarifying broad and long-term pictures; identifying one's life purpose
Ownership	Helper	Shared	Learner
Attitude to ambiguity	Eliminate it	Use it as a challenge; encourage learners to puzzle things out	Accept it as being an exciting part of the nature of the world
Use in self-development	Start where the learner is; launch; enthuse; give experiential inputs	Modelling; resolve help/control dilemma; bridge to autonomy; sup-ported reality testing	Exemplar; facilitation; integration
Benefits for the organization	Performance that is standardized, accurate and predictable	Performance that is both goal-directed and oriented towards improvements; creative solving of new problems	Conscious, questioning approach to the mission of the organization

The instructor

Good instructors plan out in detail what they want of their learners; they convey these instructions carefully, repeating key points, and encouraging note taking if appropriate; they check that the instruction has been accurately received, asking the learners to repeat back what they have been asked to do; they also check to ensure that the lesson has been put to work, and let the learners know the results.

These activities are the ones beautifully presented in the Training Within Industry (TWI) Job Instruction package. Their focus is an immediate performance of a work role. One advantage for subordinates in having a good instructor helping them is that the learners are never left in any doubt about what the helper wants, or where they stand. Good instructors are committed to *building the competence* of those they instruct. They want and expect accurate performance from their staff. If they get this, they have the satisfaction of a job well done, and the knowledge that they are in control of standards. The organization gets performance that is predictable and meets specification.

Examples of helpers who are instructors

- **Freda** is a manager of a unit of a contract catering company that serves the staff of a medium-sized factory and office block. Her staff are taught the details of their jobs, and are given refresher training on health, safety, hygiene and quality at regular intervals. She keeps a watchful eye on how jobs are being done and points out deviation from performance in a friendly manner. She checks how customers of her canteen find the service, and feeds back praise to her staff while taking action to remedy complaints.

  Most of her staff like her, enjoy the work and the company and have been with her for a long time. One or two younger staff resent 'her interfering ways', and find they have 'little opportunity to get on'.

- **Ahmed** is staff trainer at the country-house style training centre of a major bank. He teaches international procedures, international service appreciation and international trade finance. He prepares lesson plans very carefully, and when the trainees are carrying out exercises he patrols the classroom constantly, looking out for errors and difficulties and correcting them when they arise. He spends a lot of time visiting branches, developing trainees who have attended his courses. He likes to find out how they have been performing back at work, and explains the application of procedures that are still causing difficulty.

  Some of his trainees respect him, and most accept that he 'knows his stuff', and is 'very conscientious'. However, others find that he is a bit oppressive in his attention, and gets fussy about tiny and, to them, irrelevant points, which they would be able to work out for themselves in time. Others find his approach cold and impersonal. The fact that he spends so much time with each individual can mean that other trainees have to wait, often for quite long periods, before he gets round to visiting them.

These two examples illustrate how an instructing approach to helping, while having many advantages, also has drawbacks. Instructors can be blind to learners' needs to take responsibility for themselves, to risk, make mistakes and learn from them; such instructors can be bound up in detail and not give enough attention to results or to the career needs of their staff.

The coach In *A Manager's Guide to Coaching,* David Megginson and Tom Boydell describe coaching as:

a process in which a manager, through direct discussion and guided activity, helps a colleague to solve a problem, or to do a task better than would otherwise have been the case (p. 5).

As this definition indicates, the coach's way of helping involves exploring an opportunity or a problem together with the learner, and then enabling the learner to develop new knowledge, skills and competencies in working independently on it. The stages in the coaching process are:

- identifying the problem
- creating a forum for development
- carrying out the developmental activity
- developmental reviewing, i.e. reviewing to enhance learning, rather than to correct errors

The good coach will encourage the learner to play the maximum part in all these activities and will offer support and assistance when necessary. Often the support will come in the form of a question, or a tentative suggestion ('One thing you could try . . .'), rather than a specific proposal. However, skilful coaches recognize that learners vary in their capacity to cope with ambiguity. They therefore attempt to give learners the right mix of direction and choice, so they are not oppressed by overdirection or immobilized by open-endedness.

Facilitators can have two foci when coaching. One is improved task performance, the other is learning and development. They are concerned about how some immediate aspect of work is performed, and aim to improve this. At the same time, they are also keen that learners become more capable of solving the next problem independently. Many learners thrive on this dual sense of achievement of task and personal development. If instruction is about building competence, coaching is about *building performance*.

These benefits also apply to the coach. Coaches themselves often learn a great deal in the process of coaching. The organization gains from goal-directed performance, oriented towards improvement, and also from a creative approach to problem solving.

Examples of helpers who are coaches

- **Debjani** is an area sales manager for a microcomputer firm. She has six salespeople working in her area and a number of technical and administrative support staff.

  When she first got the job she accompanied each of her sales staff on a number of visits, on the understanding that she did nothing during the visit beyond the formalities, but after each visit the salespeople spent half an hour talking through what they were trying to do and why they thought this the right strategy. She took notes, but gave no feedback at this stage.

  When she had spent some time with all six she announced the first of what became a series of quarterly 'play away days' in a local hotel.

She spent an hour presenting her view of the goals for the area and then, through discussion, came up with an agreed area strategy. The rest of the day was focused on each salesperson saying what they could contribute to this strategy, and what needs they had. At this stage, Debjani offered her feedback and also invited comment from colleagues.

Each salesperson does at least one accompanied visit per month. All of them have a development project under way, which is reviewed monthly.

This worked fine for five of the salespeople, one of whom broke all company records and was promoted to manage another area. The sixth was a successful, easy-going salesman with a lot of contacts who had a golf handicap of four. He left shortly after she joined . . . to run a pub.

- **Alan** is a trainer in a national communications organization. He runs courses for junior managers which involve them in carrying out major projects during work time over a six-month period. He meets regularly with his trainees and pushes them to set targets to be achieved before the next meeting.

  Some of his trainees, particularly those with very long service in the organization, find his task oriented style 'very pushy' and are resentful, sometimes missing appointments, or even attempting to withdraw from the programme. Others find his confronting style helps them challenge old certainties and perform beyond expectations in a high-profile task.

These two case examples show that coaching, like instruction, has problems as well as advantages. Alan was operating in a role culture and his use of coaching to push the values of an achievement culture was often resented. Even Debjani did not win them all; and indeed talented individuals are often hard to help through coaching.

The mentor Mentors are much in vogue in the management and the training literature. Often, there is a certain vagueness about their role and contribution. In particular, what they are supposed to do often sounds very like what we have here called coaching.

We think there is a valid distinction between coaching and mentoring. While coaching builds performance, mentoring is concerned with *building a life's work*. The focus is on the learner's development. While instruction is broken down into small steps, and coaching focuses on a discrete task or project, mentoring is more diffuse and concerns helping the learner through life crises or into new stages of development. One lovely book that describes clearly the mentoring role of adult educators is Daloz's *Effective Teaching and Mentoring*, which persuasively combines examples from literature, e.g. Virgil's guidance of Dante through the Inferno, with verbatim reports of contemporary mentoring dialogues.

The process by which this is done seems to differ widely among mentors. Not all of them are patient Rogerian saints. Often they can place exacting demands on their learners and throw them into challenging situations.

Mentors, however, are not martinets. They are shrewd enough to listen closely and to relate what their learner says to some wider awareness of how the learner might be. Effective mentors often seem to have a well developed philosophy of life, and to operate on a spiritual dimension, as well as intellectually and emotionally. They ask a lot of questions and, whereas coaches focus on 'How?', mentors also ask 'Why?' They are good at linking different bits of their learners' lives—home and work, success and failure, concrete and abstract, thought and feeling, hard and soft. They are happy to consider the long term.

The outcome of this process for the learner can be perturbing; it can also lead to breakthroughs, and peak experiences, which are remembered with feeling decades later.

As with coaches, the process is not all one way and mentors learn, acquire insight and challenge alongside their learners. Often the questions the mentors face will be very different from those of the learner, but the developmental process is contagious and the mentor is not immune.

For the organization, the effects of mentoring are a little unpredictable. Sudden major improvements in performance can happen, but learners can also leave the organization if they decide that it no longer serves their purposes. If they stay, they may also have a more questioning approach to the mission of the organization.

Some organizations and professional bodies are promoting schemes of mentoring, and, at their best, they provide a system for transferring the wisdom and insight of experienced managers to those just embarking on their career. At worst, they provide induction (that is, socialization) that is hard to differentiate from instruction, in a context where this style is unlikely to be appropriate.

Examples of helpers who are mentors

- **Stephen** is a director of a public agency providing advice and training to Commonwealth countries on health matters. He is in his late 50s, and over the last ten years has recruited into the organization a series of talented young staff, often against the advice of colleagues. Sometimes, he is accused of favouritism. However, he seemed to get extraordinary results from these favourites, putting them into challenging overseas assignments, where they often found themselves managing people older and more experienced than themselves. One woman he appointed said, 'He made me realize I could do anything if I put my mind to it. He'd give me difficult work and, because I never wanted to let him down, I did it. In return he used to talk about his work and its problems. Apart from my family, he is the most important person in my life'.

- **Gina** is an independent consultant, who has a reputation for intellectual lucidity, integrity and down-to-earthness. In conversation with her, her clients often find their cosy preconceptions challenged and ripped apart. But just when they feel they cannot take any more, she acknowledges her own struggles and difficulties, and then allows lots and lots of time and space to the learners, to explore *their* world, and feel their way towards a new direction in their lives.

  Clients seem either to love her or hate her. She does not get repeat work from the latter. Sometimes those who reject her say that she was too big for them.

These examples illustrate disadvantages as well as advantages of mentoring. It is a powerful social process, and, while providing valuable opportunities, also presents difficulties which some may not currently be able to face.

The three styles and self-development

We now outline the part that each of these styles plays in self-development.

How instructing can help one-to-one self-development

In some ways instructing is the antithesis of self-development, but it has its place. It is also still perhaps the commonest style of facilitating, and we think it is important to acknowledge this and think about how instructors can encourage self-development and avoid some of the traps that our earlier examples—Ahmed and Freda—fell into. (See Figure 3.2.)

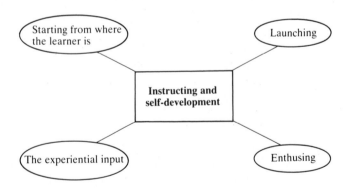

Figure 3.2 The place of instructing in self-development

Starting from where the learner is. Sometimes learners are unfamiliar with participative or learner-centred processes; they may fear and distrust teachers. One way of beginning with such a learner is to give her what she wants. If you show at the start that you can instruct competently, then, when you move on to a more demanding approach, your learner will realize that you do so from choice, not because you do not know your stuff. It is only by showing what instructing can achieve that self-directed learners will be able to recognize its shortcomings, as well as its appropriate place.

Launching.   There are areas of endeavour where initial instructing is highly functional. I will not master the intricacies of my word processing package until someone (or some manual) shows me how to get into it. Once in, I can play around and learn by myself. Before I'm in, lack of instruction breeds only frustration.

Enthusing.   A well-turned instruction delivered with conviction and ownership, is useful in both creating a vision, and encouraging.

En-thusing has an intriguing root—it comes from *en theos*—a god within. If our instructing is enthusiastic it can awaken 'that of god within each of us'. Instructing does this by providing an image of what might be (visioning) and giving fortitude and a hope of success (en-couraging) to the listener.

Next time you are planning to instruct someone, ask:

• What vision am I attempting to share?
• How will my instruction give them courage to proceed?

The experiential input.   When we give a short lecture or input, it can be a stimulus to self-development if it is characterized by:

• authenticity—saying what's true for you. If you are quoting someone else's ideas, say so, and say why these are important to you.
• ownership—if you are explaining something about the organization, take responsibility for what you see and what you do; don't blame others (the blame frame).
• doubt—if you have dilemmas, questions that are still unresolved for you, share them—your questions can inspire questions in your listeners that are relevant to their circumstances.
• open-ended—offer questions for your listener, rather than buttoning it all up for them.
• enthusiasm and vision—as we discussed earlier.
• centred on the learner—keep hold of the paradoxical notion that you are exploring your own process, in order to help your learners develop *their* issues.

Activity 3.2   Developmental instruction

Thinking about the inputs you have received which have got you going—are there any characteristics that you would like to add to this list?

• authenticity
• ownership
• doubt
• open-ended
• enthusiasm and vision
• centred on the learner

- •
- •
- •
- •
- •

Now rate yourself on all these characteristics for the last bit of instruction you gave.

I don't do this much   1   2   3   4   5   I do this well

Then use this list of characteristics as a checklist and reminder in front of you when planning and delivering your next bit of instruction.

How coaching can help one-to-one self-development

Some of the ways in which coaching helps self-development are outlined in Figure 3.3.

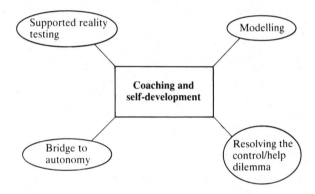

Figure 3.3 *The place of coaching in self-development*

Modelling. By exposing learners to the way in which you think, e.g. about resolving a problem, you give them the opportunity to learn about a way of doing this. However, because coaching requires shared problem solving you are encouraging them not to become clones of you, but to develop their own way, using anything of yours that seems helpful.

Resolving the control/help dilemma. Managerial coaching has elements of both control and help. Coaching is a useful mechanism, particularly for line managers wishing to encourage self-development, because it recognizes 'your need to say what must be done and to have influence on what is to be achieved, while at the same time enhancing more independent functioning' (Megginson and Boydell 1979).

The excellent coach is able to share this dilemma with the learner and monitor their mutual progress in retaining a suitable and evolving balance.

Some coaches find the language of transactional analysis useful here (Harris 1973). If you can spot parent-child, parent-parent, child-child or crossed transactions, it may help in increasing the frequency of adult-adult transactions.

Bridge to autonomy.   Many people find self-managed learning to be daunting at first. For them coaching represents a half-way house. It also provides a sense of comradeship and affiliation, which can be useful in transforming relations between managers and the people they work with. External consultants can develop a good feel for the dynamics and culture of a client organization by coaching insiders.

Supported reality testing.   'How capable am I?' is a question at once important and terrifying. Coaching provides an opportunity to generate increasingly positive answers to this question, without leaving a sense of having been pushed into a cold, shark-infested, deep end, all on your own.

As learners develop new competencies, they will *want* (or at any rate *need*) to test them out against reality.

Developing any skill or competence requires practice, and coaching provides a level of support for first steps in action, which can be particularly valuable for those learners who are strong on reflection and conceptualizing, but weaker on experimenting and experiencing.

Activity 3.3   Some questions for coaches

Thinking back on your recent coaching activities, to what extent have you:

- modelled autonomous behaviour, and encouraged people to develop their own style of finding their way through the organizational jungle?
- been clear about where you're controlling, where helping, and where leaving learners to work out things for themselves?
- encouraged discussion on issues of control, help and self-management?
- enabled the learner to test new competencies? Have you nudged a reluctant person to try new things with an agreed level of support?

Thinking forward to your next opportunity for coaching, can you use insights derived from your answers to these questions to ensure that the learning objectives of coaching have equal precedence with the organizational results you are seeking, and that the learning outcomes include learning how to learn?

How mentoring can help self-development

Mentoring can be seen as the essence of one-to-one aid for self-development. It helps this process by the three means illustrated in Figure 3.4.

Exemplar.   Mentors can help the learner by being concerned for their own self-development too. By being open, seeking feedback, learning from mistakes, asking themselves questions to clarify their own purposes, mentors can show that these processes are never-ending, and endlessly satisfying.

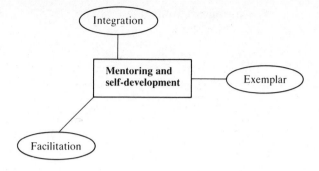

Figure 3.4 *Mentoring as a core aid to self-development*

Being truly present, aware, listening, attending to the person you are trying to help, will provide a privileged perspective on your own development. This is not because you have got it all right, but because seeing someone else's unfolding process opens up the possibility of examining your own.

Facilitation.   The core processes of mentoring:

- clarifying purpose
- active listening
- intuitive sensing
- challenging
- self-disclosure
- making sense

are key activities required for self-development. So, the effective mentor models the skills that the learner requires, and all but the most obtuse learners will notice this, and may be able to pick up these competencies or skills for themselves.

Some thoughts on developing these competencies are given later in this chapter.

Integration.   One of the ways in which a mentor helps a learner is in terms of balancing and integrating polarities (see the exercise in Chapter 2—Activity 2.14). By encouraging people to examine the space in their life allocated to:

inner — outer
work — home
public — private

mentors provide a tool for learners which may be crucial to their own self-development.

Activity 3.4 Mentoring for mentors

As a mentor you will have some ideas about how you can develop yourself. Think about the three processes below. For each one write down how you have been helped recently by someone:

- being an exemplar

- facilitating

- integrating ideas or responses

and how you could use these approaches more in your own helping:
- being an exemplar

- facilitating

- integrating ideas or responses

Skills for one-to-one self-development

Whatever style of one-to-one helping you intend to use, there will be some core processes that you will employ. These we call:
- setting goals
- diagnosing
- observing
- responding
- reviewing

We will now explore how these processes are exemplified in these three approaches to helping. Table 3.2 summarizes the core processes as competencies.

Here are some activities for developing skills in these three approaches.

Using instruction for self-development

We outline below, in a little more detail, the skills required for developmental instruction.

A Helping to clarify learner's targets.   We know from the Belbin work (1972) with older learners that adults much prefer to set their own targets rather than have them set by another. So, when setting up instruction, it is useful to give your learners a chance to set their own goals. If they are unwilling to, you may want to suggest a goal for them, or, alternatively, only start setting goals once the instructing process is well under way, and the learners have some experience on which to base their own goal setting.

Table 3.2 *Competencies used in each of the core processes according to approach to helping*

Core process	Instructing	Coaching	Mentoring
A Setting goals	Help to clarify learner's targets	Set work and learning targets	Clarify purpose
B Diagnosing	Talk through a task	Respond to doubts	Actively listen
C Presenting	Enthuse	Demonstrate competence	Self-disclosure
D Observing	Recognize skilled behaviour	Give good attention	Intuitive sensing
E Responding	Use mistakes	Give feedback	Loving challenge
F Reviewing	Encourage self-monitoring	Encourage customer review	Make sense

This is not to say that instructors should not be committed to learner success, and having very high standards for themselves. A ferocious commitment to learner achievement seems to be characteristic of the best instructors.

B Talking through the task. A practice used by many instructors, and one which encourages ownership and understanding, is to ask the learners to talk through what they are doing while practising the task they have just been instructed in. This practice is useful in ensuring that learners are not merely repeating, parrot-fashion, what they have heard, but they are really coming to grips with what the task means.

C Enthusing. One of the barriers to our being fulfilled at work is feeling that what we do is not very important. 'I can't change the world', we say. The enthusiastic instructor who loves and values the work, not only conveys skills more persuasively, but also provides the chance for the person to find meaning and direction. Valuing the mundane can add much to life. Of course, it may be that what people are asked to do is so mundane, perhaps even unnecessary, that meaning can only be found by helping the person to think more widely—about career, perhaps, or as to whether they could eliminate the job and so on. Here the role of instructor gives way to mentoring.

D Recognizing skilled behaviour. There is a special beauty in seeing a task carried out skilfully. Whether the task is programming a computer, making an omelette or playing a violin sonata, skilled performance has a number of characteristics. Argyle (1989) suggests that these are:

- smooth movement/speech
- pick up cues further ahead
- using non-verbal, sensing, tone cues as well as words and sight.

One way in which instructors can use their observational skills to help people learn is by picking out when they are missing cues—especially the less obvious cues, e.g. sound and touch in physical skills, non-verbal components of social skills. Encouraging people to watch skilled performers and notice the way they see change or trouble coming over the horizon can help this process. Video playback of the learner's performance can be a useful self-developmental tool for skill development, because the instructor often doesn't have to push lessons down learners' throats. They can see them for themselves.

E Using mistakes.   Tom Peters (1987) talks about valuing past failure, and this is another skill for instructors. If we can help people to separate out the information component from the embarrassment of making a mistake, then they are likely to be able to learn from the mistake themselves.

The instructor-of-the-year award must go to Thomas Watson Snr, the founder of IBM, who is reputed to have called someone into his office who had just made a mistake costing the company $1 000 000. When asked 'Are you going to sack me?' Watson replied 'What, when we've just invested $1 000 000 in your learning? Not likely—we need to get a return on that investment.' However, most companies can only afford a limited number of such investments.

F Encouraging self-monitoring.   'Assessment', 'judgement', 'pass/fail', 'borderline' are all words that can strike fear into our hearts. Developing a capacity for self-monitoring can help overcome these fears. Once we come to value and be confident in our self-appraisals, then judgements by others lose some of their potential for hurt.

Ideally, the skilled instructor will set up the learner's task so that the task itself provides the feedback. If this cannot be done, then it may be necessary to build in feedback from an observer. In either case, we suggest that a useful guideline is to encourage the learner to take as much control of the review process as possible.

The next activity invites you to explore how you use instruction to encourage self-development.

Activity 3.5   Instructing for self-development?

We acquire rules for what 'ought' to be done from the past, and sometimes hold onto them beyond their sell-by date. This exercise refers to Table 3.3 and encourages you to review messages you have received for each core process (Column 1) about what constitutes good traditional instruction (Column 2). Then reflect on what instructors committed to encouraging self-development in their learners would do (Column 3). Note what you currently see yourself as doing in Column 4—get feedback from anyone who has seen you in action to enrich this picture. Finally, make a note in Column 5 of goals that you might set yourself to enhance your capacity to use instruction to encourage self-development.

Table 3.3 *Core processes and instruction*

Column 1	Column 2	Column 3	Column 4	Column 5
Core process	*What good traditional instructors do*	*What self-developmental instructors do*	*What I do*	*My change goal*
A Setting goals	Set clear goals	Help to clarify learner's targets		
B Diagnosing	Test understanding	Have learner talk through the task		
C Presenting	Spell out task clearly	Enthuse		
D Observing	Check for incorrect behaviour	Recognize skilled behaviour		
E Responding	Repeat instruction as necessary	Use mistakes positively to find better way		
F Reviewing	Summarize main learning points	Encourage self-monitoring		

Using coaching to enhance self-development

Here are the skills you can use when coaching to encourage self-development.

A Setting work and learning targets. Managers using a performance management approach (Fowler 1990) will be used to setting work targets. The essence of fruitful coaching is to set work *and* learning targets. Also it can be necessary to trade the one off against the other. If Fred is the least competent writer of bills of quantities in a surveyor's office, then it may be that learning priorities demand that he take this task on, even at the expense of work performance not being maximized in the short term.

Tables 3.4 and 3.5 illustrate the difference between task goals and learning goals for a departmental manager in a cannery.

B Responding to doubts. Blaise Pascal saw doubt as an integral part of faith and we see doubt as having a crucial role in learning. When you are coaching, the cut and thrust of shared control of the process can lead enthusiastic coaches to push on through the doubts of the learner. 'Go on, give it a try. I'm with you'. From a self-development viewpoint, it may be more useful to pick up and reflect back what you see when the person seems doubtful. 'You don't look too happy about that. I'd like to hear what your concerns are' would be an alternative response.

Table 3.4 *Task goals and targets for a departmental manager*

Task goals	Task targets
Reduce overall expenditure on water by 20%, while spending not more than £10 000 on plant modification	Identify and minimize all main sources of wastage
	Review use of water and identify economies
	Review tariffs charged for water and negotiate better rates
	Identify new areas for recycling of water
	Complete implementation by next fresh produce season

Table 3.5 *Learning goal and targets for the departmental manager*

Learning goal	Knowledge targets	Skill targets	Personal developmental targets
Improved competence at complex problem solving—involving financial, negotiating and influencing skills.	Sources and volume of water wastage. Sources and volume of water use. Tariffs charged by water authorities. Areas of possible water recycling.	Improved fact-finding skills. Ability to calculate costs. Negotiation with outside bodies. Implementation of proposals with management. Clear technical report writing.	Confidence in dealing with outside bodies. Confidence in relating to senior management. Ability to handle budgets. Improved relations with engineers.

Tables 3.4 and 3.5 are adapted, with permission, from David Megginson and Tom Boydell *A Manager's Guide to Coaching*, 1979.

The benefits of this orientation will include:

- highlighting areas where the learner may need further development, information or courage
- identifying difficulties and blockages that you hadn't noticed yourself, thus increasing *your* learning
- building trust and respect into the relationship.

C Demonstrating competence.   On the other hand, there will be occasions when the coach has a great deal of information, insight, contacts, or background which will be inefficient and frustrating for learners to pick up for themselves. On these occasions it may be appropriate to use or convey this wisdom directly to the learner.

From a self-development point of view, the following suggestions may help:

- If you are fixing things with other people, do it in the presence of the learner.
- If you are explaining 'how things are', use personal language—'from my point of view', 'I see the key person we have to convince is . . .'. This creates the possibility of learners expressing their own views without having to contradict yours directly.
- Ask for your learner's *comments* and *thoughts* (rather than simply *questions*) when you've finished.

D Giving good attention. Harvey Jackins (1973) says that everyone in the world just wants to be listened to, but they seldom get what they want, because so does everybody else.

Giving attention, space, friendly eye contact is a precious gift.

Activity 3.6 Attention!

To develop this fundamental and crucial skill we suggest that you practise the basic co-counselling process of giving good attention. It is an exercise for which you will require a partner. The process is as follows:

1 Decide who will be the listener and who the speaker first. The speaker thinks up a topic he or she is currently working on, and has not yet satisfactorily resolved. If both listener and speaker are work colleagues, it could be the kind of topic they might seek coaching on.
2 The speaker then has five minutes to explore the topic and see what kind of sense he or she can make of it. The speaker is encouraged to use this time for personal use *for themselves*. The task is not to explain the position to the listener. Rather, the listener offers the speaker the gift of attention, as a support for the speaker's own deliberations.
3 While the speaker is going strong, the listener maintains eye contact, remains alert to what the speaker is saying, and *does nothing* other than listen. If the speaker does hesitate, or gets stuck, the listener can:

   - smile and/or nod encouragingly
   - say 'Mmmm' or 'Go on'
   - repeat verbatim a phrase from what the speaker has just said.

   If none of these helps, the speaker is asked to summarize where he or she has got to, and what he or she wants to explore next. For the exercise to have a chance to work it is important that the speaker *does nothing else*. If the speaker stays stuck, then just remain with them in companionable silence. The speaker will probably restart, and if this does not happen, you will have only a couple of minutes left. The silence may even be useful.
4 When the time is up, ask the speaker to review briefly how he or she felt, and have the listener comment on anything in the speaker which was noticed that confirms the speaker's feelings.
5 Swap roles and repeat stages 1 to 4. This sharing of time is a crucial part of the co-counselling process. It is less important for our purposes. However, it is worth doing, to establish a sense of reciprocity and sharing for the discussion to follow. It is also useful for coaches

to have the experience that simply being listened to can be helpful in thinking an issue through.

6 When you have both had a go, brainstorm together a list of all the verbal and non-verbal behaviours of the listener in both parts of the activity. For each behaviour, ask the speaker who witnessed it to say whether it was:
   • an unhelpful, non-attending behaviour, or
   • an unhelpful, attending behaviour (you were getting so much attention it was intimidating), or
   • a helpful, attending behaviour.

7 After this discussion, look at Table 3.6, below, and compare your list with ours.

8 Review what actions this activity has suggested for you as a coach.

Table 3.6   *Non-attending and attending behaviours*

Some unhelpful, non-attending behaviours

• looking away from the other person; looking around the room; staring down in front of you
• doodling on a piece of paper
• fidgeting with objects on your desk
• using your desk as a protective barrier
• closing your eyes
• yawning
• looking at your watch
• sitting too far away from the other person
• sitting sideways on to the other person, or at an awkward angle to him

Some unhelpful attending behaviours

• staring hard at the other person all the time; fixing him with an unwavering glare
• frowning, scowling, looking stern
• overaggressively leaning forward towards the other person, in a tense, threatening manner
• sitting too close to the other person
• interrupting

Some helpful attending behaviours

• sitting facing the other person, without any physical barriers in between
• maintaining helpful eye contact; looking directly at the other person, without fixing him with a frightening stare
• leaning slightly forward towards the other person
• maintaining a relaxed posture
• using encouraging responses, e.g. nodding, 'mming', saying things like: 'I understand', 'I see what you mean'.

Table 3.6 is adapted, with permission, from David Megginson and Tom Boydell, *A Manager's Guide to Coaching*, 1979.

E Giving feedback.   Neville Ward (1986) says of giving negative feedback:

It is possible to make an unbiased adverse judgement about another person, but it needs great skill. It is extremely difficult to make a strictly unbiased criticism of someone unless you do in fact love that human being and wish them nothing but good. Two factors account for the difficulty; they are distressingly frequent; one is the secret intent to hurt, the other is the desire for superiority.

(Friday Afternoon, p. 20)

Ward's perspective encourages us to examine our inner motives because:

If we have demands on life that have not been met . . . if at times we play around rather long with despair, there is bound to be lurking in the hinterland of our personalities the desire to hit out at life. However successful we are at controlling that desire we shall not prevent its giving just that corrupting touch of hostility to all our critical judgements by which they cease to be expressions of disinterested opinion and become vehicles of our stored-up bitterness, weapons to serve us in our secret, sullen struggle with a world we are against.

(pp. 20–1)

And again:

Even if we have no need to raise ourselves in the opinion of others we may yet wish to feel rather more assured in our own opinion. To sum up things and people and make discerning judgements about them always leaves a slight feeling of power, and silences for the moment the sense of inferiority.

(p. 21)

The skills of giving feedback, then, are not merely technical ones (start from strengths, speak from the 'I', don't judge the person, be specific, say what you want to happen), valuable though these ideas are. They also reach down deeply into our selves and demand of us humility, self-assurance and caution.

F Encouraging customer review.   When we are trying things out and are still uncertain of our abilities, we can be reluctant to find out how we are doing. So people may find it hard to go beyond the coaching relationship to seek feedback. It can help them if we encourage this.

Coaching has work goals as well as learning ones. It is important to both sets of goals that work attainment is tested out quickly with as many interested parties as possible. Encouraging learners to do this review on the coaching activity will help them to incorporate this into all their work.

Activity 3.7   Drawing together

Activity 3.7 offers a challenging and intriguing way of exploring the work and learning relationship between coach and learner.

It uses the metaphor of drawing simultaneously on a piece of paper to explore the issues that may be alive for you and the other person. It can be done with a colleague, but clearly it has a special power and potential if you can use it to explore an actual coaching relationship. The act of drawing—getting away from verbal forms where most of us are most comfortable—highlights issues that might not otherwise come to light.

This process can be enhanced if you do the drawing part of the activity in silence.

Step 1   Assemble a large sheet of plain paper, somewhere between A3 and a flip-chart sheet in size, and a range of coloured pens or crayons—just one of each colour.

Step 2   Explain that the purpose of the exercise is to draw a shared picture. The picture will describe your work relationship. You will draw it simultaneously, starting from opposite sides of the paper. It can be representational or metaphoric. The aim is to make *one* picture to which you both contribute, so your efforts will need to merge in some way. The exercise is best done in silence. If you draw people, it is best not to put in bubbles with words coming out of their mouths. Try to express what they want to communicate in the drawing. Needless to say, artistic merit is not the aim. Our drawing is a tool for exploring and expressing ideas and feelings.

Step 3   Carry out the activity allowing enough time to fill the picture, and continue till both parties have drawn enough to satisfy themselves. Who starts first and who completes the picture may raise interesting debating points about the way you work together.

Step 4   Allow plenty of time for the debrief—a minimum of half an hour. Start by taking it in turns to share what went on for you during the drawing, and indeed before and after. Describe how it was for you in terms of:

- **thinking**: what ideas you had, where they came from, how they developed during the drawing, images or notions you had about yourself or your co-drawer.
- **feeling**: what you felt, in terms of enjoyment/distaste, power/helplessness, collaboration/competition or whatever else came up for you. Bear in mind the principle that whatever you or your colleague felt is more usefully considered to be something about you rather than about the other party. So if, for example, at some stage you felt aggrieved or really angry with the other person, tell them the feeling, and then describe what it is in you that makes you susceptible to such feelings. This is more likely to be productive than attempting to blame the other party for giving you such a bad time.
- **willing**: what actions you took, what actions you wanted to take but restrained yourself, when you initiated, when responded to the other's initiative.

It can be helpful if each person has a few minutes to outline their thinking, feeling and willing to the other, with a ground rule that the other does not interrupt, except for purposes of clarification.

Step 5 Having shared thoughts, feelings and impulses to action, make a list or draw a string bag (see Figure 2.2, page 34) of the issues that this raises for one or other or both of you for your coaching relationship. Treat this as a shared task to be done together, but do include items that are relevant for only one of you.

Step 6 Bearing in mind the time you have left, pick a number of issues that are important to each of you (perhaps taking it in turns like the dreadful ritual of picking teams in the school playground). Then work through these issues, coming up with agreed action points for each. Note these in Table 3.7 below and each of you take a copy. Agree a date for follow-up review.

Table 3.7 *Drawing together—action plan*

Issue	Coach's actions	Learner's actions

Mentoring—a royal road to self-development

The whole process of mentoring is a key mechanism for enabling the self-development of others. Badly handled it can turn into an anti-developmental process. The skills listed below seem to us to be important ones in preventing negative mentoring—which, at worst, can seem like an attempt to take over another's life and to relive it vicariously, grasping at the chances that have been missed in the mentor's own career.

The core self-developmental skills and competencies are:

A Clarifying purpose Sometimes, especially at the start of a mentoring relationship, we may find people citing goals to please the mentor, but which are miles away from what they actually want.

Example Duncan, an undergraduate coming to the end of his first year of a single honours science degree, after poor exam results, is asked by the science faculty tutor 'Given the choice of any course in the university, what would you like to do next year?' Duncan replies, after brief thought, 'Economics and psychology', but he is looking down and his voice lacks sparkle or conviction. The science tutor says 'Have you chosen those because they're the two most liberal science courses?' A nod. 'Then look through the whole university prospectus and choose what you'd really like'. Duncan chooses second and third year philosophy courses, English first and second year courses, and stays with the economics. He goes on to negotiate entry to these courses and successfully completes his course.

Attending to non-verbal cues is important in this area, but also more central is the ability to face up to purpose and purposelessness in life and to ask the basic if daunting questions:

- Why are you here?
- What do you want to be known for when you've retired?
- What is your life purpose?
- What do you want to achieve more than anything else in the world?

We all need help in responding to these!

B Listening actively   To clarify purpose, we also need this skill. Being silent and attentive is part of active listening, but in addition there is a need for sensing the music beneath the words. Try this process with a trusted friend or colleague.

Activity 3.8   Active listening

Have your partner talk about some matter of importance to them. Listen and attend to what is said on the surface. Also notice feelings and impulses that you guess might be floating just under the surface, and from time to time interpolate a question beginning 'Could it be . . .?' For example, 'Could it be that you're not as happy about this as you say?' or 'Could it be that this would be a compromise for you?' Whether your partner accepts or refutes your implied suggestion, no matter. Sometimes the comments closest to the bone will be the most staunchly rebuffed.

But after both of you have had a turn, go over the questions each asked, and see, candidly, if there was anything in them. A tape or video recorder helps with this activity.

C Self-disclosure   One of the things that helps a group develop is building in opportunities for self-disclosure. If people are open, then the group gets going. Sidney Jourard, the American psychologist, demonstrated how self-disclosure by one individual encourages it in others. This is important for mentoring.

If, as a mentor, you can appropriately disclose your own process, thoughts, feelings and concerns, then you create a forum where it is safe for another to do the same. Of course, it is important to remember that premature or overdone self-disclosure may have the opposite effect and shut people up. For example, it is perhaps better to describe some current, real dilemma in your own life, rather than saying 'When I was your age, I had a real problem deciding what I wanted to do'.

D Intuitive sensing This takes deeper the process we describe above as active listening. At this level, rather than rely on subtle non-verbal or verbal cues, we stay open to the whole of our awareness, and see what comes up. Maybe when our learner is talking with us an image will arise, rather like a dream, only we are awake and aware. If the image comes to us, the suggestion is: don't filter it to see if it makes sense, but offer it to the learner to see if it makes sense to them.

E Loving challenge Sometimes we don't respond to feedback, listening, self-disclosure, even the offering of the fruits of another's intuition. In these cases, a challenge may be called for—confronting a person with their blind spots or inappropriate actions is a response that risks jeopardizing the relationship in attempting to interrupt a deeply ingrained pattern in the learner.

Example In Shakespeare's *Julius Caesar*, Cassius and Brutus before the battle of Philippi are in difficult circumstances, and the cool, rational Brutus challenges the headstrong, impulsive Cassius. Cassius is mortified and says accusingly 'I thought you loved me', to which Brutus replies with 'I love you, but not your faults'.

This kind of challenge, though risky, is possible in friendships and partnerships. Almost, we might say, it defines the difference between a deep friendship and an acquaintanceship. This is valuable as a sparingly used intervention in a mentoring relationship.

F Making sense If the first skill of mentoring is clarifying purpose, the last has parallels in that, having mapped out the road and explored various turnings, we are now ready to explore what it all means.

When asked what we have learned, particularly from calamities that have befallen us, we often say something like 'I've learned not to make that mistake again' or 'I've seen that I should never associate with such people again'. Making sense takes us beyond the 'should', beyond the narrow and the negative.

When we invite people to make sense of their experience we are encouraging them to explore beyond their current level of awareness, possibly confronting their next developmental stage.

Table 3.8 is a summary of developmental stages culminating with the issues that mentors can help learners look at in order to move onto the next developmental step.

The exercise that rounds off our consideration of mentoring and this chapter is a visualization activity. You can carry it out alone either by reading the instructions, and giving yourself space to think about them before reading on, or by reading the instructions into a tape recorder, with suitable silences, and then playing it back. Alternatively, you can get someone to read it out for you. Have pen and paper handy. It is best done sitting down.

Table 3.8 *Developmental stages, benefits, blockages, and questions to ask*

Developmental stage or mode	Benefits of this way of managing	Effect of being blocked at this stage	Nature of next developmental step
1 Rules and procedures	Set procedures etc. can be of use in certain types of emergency, where it is particularly important to do the 'right' thing quickly and correctly. They are also useful for beginners, because they can provide a reassuring base from which to start.	In fact, not many managers are stuck at this stage. Those that are can only operate in a limited number of 'standard' situations, and are likely to be most ineffective at anything that might be described as 'truly managerial'.	To move on, you need to start querying, modifying or deviating from standard procedures, seeking explanations and reasons rather than mere instructions.
2 Norms and conventions *Influenced mainly by external factors*	Enables you to behave in an 'appropriate' way— i.e. in the way that is in accord with accepted reasons, rationales and explanations, and is socially and politically respectable. In so doing you are likely to be popular with the powers that be, keeping your nose clean and being considered safe, acceptable and reliable.	Many managers remain at this stage, and are quite happy to do so, since it can lead to a reasonably content existence. On the other hand, these managers are likely to find any unexpected change most unpleasant and difficult to cope with. Should they be forced to leave the organization (e.g. through redundancy) they will have a particularly bad time adjusting to their new situation. Also, of course, there is often a long-term price to be paid for not being oneself—a certain malaise, doubt, 'surely there's more to life than this?' begins to creep in. They suffer from all the effects of not managing themselves—i.e. they are stuck, become bored, lazy, timeservers etc.	You need to start questioning and challenging the established and accepted ways and reasons for doing things. Start to think for yourself: do you really think this is the best way of doing something? Is this really a good, acceptable or valid explanation or reason? How can you find out for yourself, come to your own conclusion or decision?
3 Thinking for yourself	Much more likely to be creative, and to be able to manage new ambiguous, changing situations, both within your organization and in other aspects	Being stuck at this stage means that you are so keen on thinking for yourself that you become too self-directing, completely ignoring the ideas,	You need, therefore, to start to temper your arrogance with humility, and to synthesize or combine self-management with management by and

Developmental stage or mode	Benefits of this way of managing	Effect of being blocked at this stage	Nature of next developmental step
Enter the self: now internal factors have a big influence	of your life. Also greater feelings of self-confidence and self-worth. The price to pay for this is that you may well be unpopular at times with those who like to maintain the status quo and do things in the 'proper' manner.	feelings, values and goals of other people, and the effect of your actions on them. You are also likely to distort your confidence into a form of arrogance.	of other people; particularly by becoming aware of their views etc., and of the effect of your actions on them before coming to your final decision. It is also useful at this stage to start thinking about what you have to offer others, to contribute to their development.
4 Awareness *Now it's both internal and external factors, in a synthesis of the two*	You are now thinking for yourself, making your own decisions etc. in full awareness both of yourself and of others and their goals, ideas, feelings; this leads to what is often seen as 'intuitive behaviour'. To do this involves '. . . both . . . and' thinking, and requires open-mindedness and suspension of judgement; in addition, of course, this awareness enables you to choose which of these modes to operate in—i.e. you now have a repertoire available to you, from which you can choose consciously. Thus, this is the stage of effective management.	Not a bad stage to be 'stuck' at! However, you may now find an increasing need and desire to use these skills, this ability to manage yourself, to a particular purpose, that you yourself feel to be important. There is also a danger of abusing these abilities, this high level of consciousness, to further personal ambition, manipulate others and gain power over them, or for other negative, evil ends.	Start to look for this special purpose: ask, 'Why on earth am I here? What am I doing with my life?'
5 Purpose *Now you apply this synthesis, this art of managing yourself to a particular purpose—to your purpose in life*	Now you are managing yourself with a full awareness of your purpose in life, of the task you want to achieve. Hopefully this task isn't something just for yourself, but in some way makes a definite contribution to the development of your organization, profession, area of expertise, community, affinity group, family, or whatever it is that you choose to commit yourself to. However, there is also a great danger that this commitment will be to some negative or evil cause—this is where we find fanatics, despots, tyrants (sometimes obvious, sometimes posing as great saviours).		

Source: Reproduced, with permission, from Mike Pedler and Tom Boydell *Managing Yourself*, Fontana (1985), pp. 70–1.

Activity 3.9   Visualize yourself as a mentor

These instructions are for you to read out to yourself, or to have read out by someone else.

Sit somewhere comfortable. Loosen tight clothing. Relax your body. Unlock arms, legs. If you are sitting, place each foot squarely on the ground. (Pause)

Notice your breathing. Let it get slower, deeper, feeling the breath as you breathe in, and then feeling it, soft and warm, as you breathe out. (Pause)

Now build an image of yourself as you are now in your mentoring. (Pause) If your image is of you, notice how you sit, how you talk, how you listen. (Pause) Notice how your learner relates to you and how you respond to this. (Pause) If you have an image of yourself, other than your human shape, notice what this is, and how you feel about it. Notice how the other responds to this form. What does this make you feel? (Pause)

Imagine you hear two people talking about you as a mentor. One knows you only slightly and starts telling the other about your reputation. You hear what they say. (Pause)

Then the other, who knows you better, talks of your hidden strengths that emerge with longer acquaintance, and your limitations. (Pause) You recall what they said and your own image of you as a mentor and, remaining relaxed, note down any points you need to recall. (Pause)

Now, when you are ready, imagine a wise mentor, an expert who can use their own experience and deep wisdom to be a helpful, liberating, transforming guide to others. (Pause) It may be someone you know, or an imaginary figure. It may be an aspect of you, accessing your own inner wisdom. (Pause) Now, imagine yourself stepping into that wise mentor's shoes. Imagine yourself becoming the insightful guide who knows how to be a mentor. Imagine this guide being clear about how to mentor, and spelling out with lucid enthusiasm how you can use your skills, experience, qualities and opportunities to become a fully effective mentor. (Pause) Listen to what the wise mentor says, and, when you are ready, note this down. (Pause) When you are ready, and not before, stop writing, thank the mentor for the strong image of how you might be, and come back into awareness of your surroundings. (Pause) Look around. (Pause) Move about a bit. (Pause)

Then, when you are ready, take your notes of how you are now, and how you might be, and see what lessons there are for you here in developing yourself as a mentor.

References

Argyle, M. (1989) *The Social Psychology of Work* (2nd ed.), Penguin, Harmondsworth.

Belbin, E. and R. M. (1972) *Problems in Adult Retraining*, Heinemann, London.

Daloz, L. A. (1986) *Effective Teaching and Mentoring*, Jossey-Bass, San Francisco.

Fowler, A. (1990) 'Performance management: the MBO of the '90s?' *Personnel Management*, 22(7), pp. 47–51.

Jackins, H. (1973) *The human situation*, Rational Island, Seattle.

Harris, T. (1973) *I'm OK: You're OK*, Pan, London.

Megginson, D. and T. Boydell (1979) *A Manager's Guide to Coaching*, BACIE, London.

Pedler, M. and T. Boydell (1985) *Managing Yourself*, Fontana, London.

Peters, T. (1987) *Thriving on Chaos*, Macmillan, London.

Ward, J. N. (1986) *Friday Afternoon*, Epworth, London.

4 Working with groups

In this chapter we move away from considering our work with individuals to look at how we can encourage self-development in groups. To do this, we examine three processes analogous to instructing, coaching and mentoring in the previous chapter. We call these *directing, guiding* and *enabling*. And we look at these processes in relation to three sorts of groups that we have often found to be levers for development in organizations:

- **management teams**—where team building is required, and a fair amount of *directing* may be seen as appropriate;
- **action learning sets**—where *guidance* is called for, to link the doing of work to the learning about self, others and organization;
- **self-development groups**—where the strongly self-determining group often requires a lighter touch, and the role of the developer is to *enable* participants to take on group functions for themselves.

The part of the developer's diamond field that we are focusing on is highlighted in Figure 4.1.

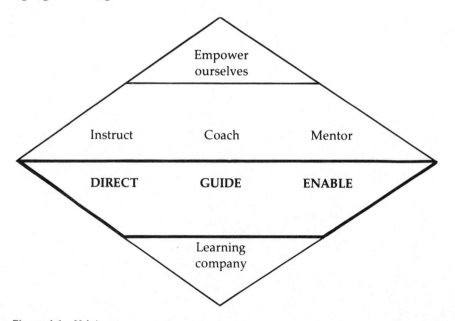

Figure 4.1 *Helping groups*

Why self-development in groups?

It may seem paradoxical to write a chapter about groups in a book about the apparently individual process of self-development. In practice, however, do-it-yourself self-development is a lonely and disconcertingly ineffective process. In one D-I-Y programme we were involved with, only 10 per cent of participants made significant progress. It seems that, for most people, the feedback, support and challenge of others is a crucial part of their individual development. This is where groups can be so useful.

An advantage of working with groups is that it is possible to move from the potentially regressive relationship between helper and helped, towards a peer relationship between what Reg Revans describes as 'comrades in adversity' (Revans 1983). Many of the activities in this chapter are designed to contribute to that movement. They are about you making space, encouraging and enabling group members to work skilfully with each other.

Three types of groups and their characteristics

We differentiate in Table 4.1 the types of groups we will be exploring.

Table 4.1   *Characteristics of types of groups*

Type of group	Team building	Action learning set	Self-development group
How people join	Obligated	Sponsored	Free will
Focus	Task, working together	Work problem, self	Self, life and career
Facilitator role	Directing—provide structure, exercises and process review	Guiding—provide structure and process review	Enabling—initiate structure and process review
Format	Concentrated, with periodic follow-up reviews	Regular half-day meetings over about 6 months	Regular one-day meetings over a year or more

Team building

Team building is a process by which members of an organization who have a common boss, meet together with that boss to develop their team functioning. They often do this by addressing real work issues directly, and team building therefore resembles an ordinary work meeting more strongly than other kinds of group development. However, it does differ from an everyday meeting in having a facilitator present. This person helps the group to review the process by which it carries out its tasks, and to learn from the experience.

An outcome of team building will often be a commitment to an agreed plan of action, and this may require review meetings to explore progress.

These reviews may also be useful as a forum for evaluating the success of the team building. Evaluation can also be done, however, against quantified performance targets set by the work group, or organizational targets established for them.

Action learning sets

Action learning sets (see Revans 1983; Pedler 1991) are an approach to integrating the often separated worlds of work and learning. They provide a setting for each participant to discuss and learn about a real, major and urgent work problem which demands resolution, and which they are charged with resolving. The problem may be connected to their own job, or to a job in a different part of the organization or, indeed, a different organization. It may concern the function with which they are familiar, or another function. Increasingly, in recent years, the action learning problem may have strategic or cross-functional implications.

Entry to an action learning set is usually sponsored. In other words, members' applications have been endorsed by their line managers, a mentor, or human resource management.

The focus of work in the sets is on a specific and tangible work problem. The principal support and challenge comes from fellow participants, as does specialist advice and know-how about aspects of the problem. The facilitator, or action learning set adviser, helps by guiding the group towards the establishment of a mode of operating, and by drawing the group's attention to issues that will enable the group to work more effectively.

Action learning programmes usually last around six months, with set meetings held at least monthly, sometimes more frequently. Whereas team-building meetings must have as many members as there are in the team, action learning sets are best kept within the range of five to eight members.

Evaluation is by the successful resolution of work problems, and an initial assessment of this success is often made by the set and members of senior management attending a final day session to round off the formal action learning process. Work on implementation of solutions and informal group contact may, of course, continue after this date. It is also an important part of evaluation to review the learning that participants have achieved in working together on their own and each other's problems. Finally, it is a part of action learning's evaluation to assess members' capacity to learn how to learn.

Self-development groups

All three types of group embody a wide variety of experience, depending on membership, current issues, facilitator interests and so on. Not only is each group unique, but each participant's experience will also differ from all the others. So, what we say about these groups, and particularly self-development groups, is not a recipe. Rather, it is a chart of our experiences, offering some landmarks that have given us a perspective and a direction when travelling over this complex and varied terrain.

One thing that does not vary is the importance for self-development groups of having members who are genuine volunteers. Even here there will be degrees of voluntariness, and in some organizational cultures it will be usual for members to be sponsored or even for gentle pressure to be put on potential participants to encourage them to explore the possibility of self-development. It is crucial, though, that participants be given the freedom afforded to the fabled horse, who, however firmly it was led to the water, still had the option of whether or not to drink.

The focus of self-development groups is often quite diffuse, particularly at the beginning. Some participants want to acquire theoretical knowledge—about motivation or delegation, for instance. Others want specific information about the organization, e.g. on facilities for counselling or how the disciplinary procedure works. Yet others may already be thinking about their own work needs—How can I deal with this difficult staff member?   How can I get my boss to listen to me? And others may be considering their careers, and what their next step might be—what they want from life. We have found that a valuable staff role is to help to provide space for the expression and meeting of all these needs, so that the group may determine its own way forward, rather than being led by the enthusiasms of the facilitator. This enabling role requires a light touch, and a confidence in the potential and wisdom inherent in the group. Can it be developed still further?

Three types of group and self-development

In this section we outline our understanding of how team building, action learning sets and self-development groups can be established to contribute most effectively to the goals of self-development. We will then go on to identify ways of developing some skills useful in facilitating the three types of group. Finally we explore 'making space'—a core skill in enhancing self-development in groups.

What is team building?

Prescriptive models for team building

Much that is written about team building prescribes a model for what a good team should be like. This approach rather goes against the tenets of self-development, where we encourage teams to determine their own goals and direction. However, these models do have the advantage of providing a framework of certainty within which a team may experiment without being overwhelmed by ambiguity.

If you do want to use such a model, one we have found useful is the work of Larson and LaFasto (1989), whose research indicted that successful teams had the following characteristics:

- clear, elevating goal
- results-driven structure

- competent team members
- unified commitment
- collaborative climate
- standards of excellence
- external support and recognition
- principled leadership

Activity 4.1 is based on Larson and LaFasto's model—we have turned it into a self-exploration mode by posing many of their issues as questions. To diagnose the workings of a team you are associated with, members could go through the questions related to the eight characteristics, as pre-work before attending a team-building event. The event could then be structured around their responses to the questions, which could be used to set priorities for action and an agenda for that action.

Activity 4.1   Some questions about team functioning

1   A clear, elevating goal

- To what extent is your team goal clearly stated?
- Is the goal personally and collectively challenging?
- Does the goal create a sense of urgency—would achieving it make a difference?
- Do politics and personal agenda get in the way of people focusing on the goal?

2   Results-driven structure

- Does the team structure contribute to the desired results?
- Are there clear roles and accountability?
- Is there an effective communication system within the team?
- Is individual performance monitored and feedback provided?

3   Competent team members

- Are team members selected because they are the best for the job?
- In selecting people, are technical and personal skills both taken into account?
- Do members' personal characteristics match the nature of the team task?
- Do staff have a strong desire to contribute?
- Are they capable of collaborating effectively?
- Is the team self-correcting in the face of challenges?

4   Unified commitment

- Are team members dedicated to the team's endeavour?
- Do they identify closely with the team itself?
- Are team members involved in clarifying strategies for achieving the team goal, or even in defining that goal?

5   Collaborative climate

- Do the members work well together?

- Are relationships characterized by:
  —trust
  —openness
  —consistency
  —respect?
- Is trust built by members being given involvement and autonomy?

6 Standards of excellence

- Is there high pressure to perform, from:
  —individuals
  —the team
  —the consequences of success or failure
  —external pressure
  —the team leader?
- Is there a concrete commitment to *meeting* standards, as well as setting them?
- Do members resist, ignoring standards when they become difficult to achieve?
- Are standards clearly and concretely articulated?
- Does the team strive constantly to improve standards?

7 External support and recognition

- Does the team receive both support in principle and the resources it needs?
- Do team members receive tangible rewards for their achievements?

8 Principled leadership

- Does the leader establish a clear vision for the team?
- Does the leader generate change away from the *status quo*?
- Does the leader unleash talent?
- Does the leader suppress his/her own ego and encourage others to do the same?
- Does the leader create leaders rather than followers?

Activity 4.1 provides a way of generating an agenda in which both team leader and team members can engage equally. However, the sharp difference in roles between leader and members can mean that the goals of self-development are more fruitfully pursued if the members are given an opportunity to set the agenda. In the next section we discuss an intriguing design for team building that has this advantage.

Team building—a developmental approach

There are a number of obstacles to making team building a developmental event for the manager of the team. First, the facilitator needs a light hand so that her role does not become too dominant. Second, in many organizations, learning from one's staff is countercultural. Third, processes that lead to development may be at odds with the relatively strongly task-oriented group process that can develop in a team-building event.

The international strategy implementation consultancy—the Forum Corporation—has devised a valuable means of getting round these barriers, described as 'upward feedback'.

The essence of upward feedback is that the staff of the line manager have the first say, by giving collective feedback to their boss around the boss's performance on a number of key practices that have been identified as critical to success in their organization.

This process is described in the example below.

Example   **The Forum approach to upward feedback**

Assumption:
Detailed and accurate feedback is instrumental in adult learning.

Process:
1 The organization members decide what practices are required to enable a certain organizational outcome.
2 A feedback questionnaire is created and distributed to the staff or peers of the manager.
3 These are filled out, sent to Forum, processed by Forum.
4 Adviser gives the feedback report to the manager.
5 The adviser meets with the manager to help him/her 'size up' the feedback and prepare a meeting with his/her team to clarify the feedback.
6 The adviser may play a facilitative role in the team meeting.
7 The adviser meets with the manager to debrief the team meeting and enable the manager to commit to a developmental action plan.
8 The manager works with his/her manager on including this plan into the performance objectives.

In Forum's recent work with one of its corporate clients, BP Exploration, it found that the 'upward feedback' method of team building not only led to some excellent focused action planning for individual teams, but it also contributed to 'developing a style and climate which liberates the talents, enthusiasm and commitment of all our people'—in the words of BP chairman, Robert Horton. It has the advantage of enhancing 'the upward communication of doubt' (Revans 1983), which we discuss later in this chapter. The feedback process does this by giving the responsibility for generating the issues to be addressed firmly to the team. They fill out a questionnaire about their manager in which they specify, against a list of practices identified as crucial to developing the company's style, how important each practice is to them, and the extent to which they see their manager as executing that practice. The manager then receives, for each practice, an averaged score on how the team see its importance and his/her execution of it.

An added advantage of this instrumented approach to team building is that it is very time-efficient, the meetings between manager, facilitator and team taking, typically, only four hours. This feature is valuable, because it then makes feasible the possibility of running team building for every manager in the organization, even one the size of BP Exploration. They found that this had a powerful cumulative effect, where, for example, at a senior manager's 'upward feedback', one of his team said 'At *my* feedback, my team were saying the same thing to me, so it's not just something that affects you as the overall boss, it's something that we all need to address'.

Some of the skills of running team building in a self-developmental way are explored later in this chapter, but first we examine the other group approaches to self-development.

A summary handout by Kath Aspinwall answering the question 'What is action learning?' is shown below.

Action learning sets

What is action learning?

Action Learning is an approach to management education developed by Revans, based on his premise that 'there can be no learning without action and no (sober and deliberate) action without learning' (Revans 1983, p.54). Revans suggests that organisations (and those within them) cannot survive or flourish unless the rate of learning is equal to, or greater than, the rate of change they are experiencing ($L > C$). He describes learning as having two elements, traditional instruction or programmed knowledge, and critical reflection or questioning insight, and proposes the learning equation, $L = P + Q$. He also distinguishes between puzzles and problems. 'Puzzles' have 'best' solutions and can be solved by the application of programmed knowledge with the help of experts. 'Problems' are more complex and are dealt with by different individuals in different ways. In this context, questioning insight plays a critical role. Programmed knowledge can be, and is, sought but only after careful reflection on what knowledge is needed and why.

Action Learning Groups bring together small groups of managers with the following intentions:

- to undertake to work on and through management problems. This must be a voluntary commitment.
- to work on real problems with which they are actively engaged. Situations in which 'I am part of the problem and the problem is part of me'.
- to work together to check individual perceptions, clarify (and render more manageable) the problem, and to explore alternatives for action.
- to take action in the light of new insight. This will begin to change the situation and an account of the consequences will be brought back to the group for further shared reflection.
- to focus on learning, not only about the problem being tackled but also on what is being learned about oneself. This is essential if developing understanding is to become learning and thus be transferable to other situations.
- to be aware of group processes and develop effective ways of working together. Each group is provided with a facilitator whose role is to help the group to identify and develop the necessary skills.
- to provide the balance of support and challenge which will enable each individual to manage more effectively.

Reproduced by permission of the author, Kath Aspinwall, October 1990.

Activity 4.2   Start an action learning set

To start an action learning set:

1 Recruit six or so people who wish to develop themselves through tackling a live company problem, e.g. increasing quality, cutting waste, improving a service.
2 Ask each person to write a brief description of the problem to be tackled and a picture of how things will be when it is resolved—what benefits will result?
3 For each person find a sponsor or mentor who can act as a company aunt or uncle, smoothing the path, giving advice and so on.
4 Agree a schedule—say half a day every two weeks or a day every month—for the group to meet, perhaps with a set adviser to help manage the process and encourage members to give and take between themselves.
5 At each meeting members share time and report in turn on their efforts since the last meeting. Other members help each person to learn from their actions by questions and feedback, support and challenge. Finally, each person ends by setting goals for action to be carried out by the next meeting.

This is a simple yet profound process. Only individuals prepared to take a risk and commit themselves to action and reflection will be able to learn in this way. Only organizations open to learning will allow members this sort of freedom. Action learning is one of the most powerful methods of development to emerge in the 1970s and 80s. You can make it part of a more extensive course, or you can have sets freestanding. These days it is quite hard to find a well-designed development programme without at least an action learning component.

Action learning develops the quality of 'questioning insight' in people and companies, in the belief that 'doubt ascending creates wisdom from above', to quote one of Revans' golden sayings. Of course, the organization has to be ready for this, otherwise there is a danger of 'doubt ascending bringing retribution from above', as a cynical colleague of ours says!

Self-development groups— the direct route to growth?

We have put a question mark at the end of the title of this section because, in one sense, self-development groups address issues of development more directly than team building and action learning sets, but in another sense they do not. Clearly, their focus is directly upon the members' development, so from the start this agenda is legitimized. On the other hand, one of the characteristics of these groups is that their initial process will involve a fair amount of apparently directionless wandering about. So, in some senses, self-development groups are a direct method; in other senses, they can be infuriatingly indirect.

In Chapter 2 we described setting up a self-development group for *your own* development. In this chapter our concern is with setting up self-development groups for others. Most of what we say refers to establishing groups in the context of a single organization. However, it has relevance to other contexts, such as open access programmes and consortia of several small firms. Open access self-development groups are often focused on whole-life issues, and may be called biography groups (see, for example, Janice and Malcolm Leary, 'Transforming your career', Chapter 10 of Pedler, Burgoyne and Boydell 1988). Consortia have often been established under the aegis of the Employment Department's schemes, which in recent years have been called Local Collaborative Projects and Business Growth Training. For the rest of this section, though, we shall be writing as if the self-development group or groups you will be setting up are located in a single organization.

Because self-development groups are the freest form in our spectrum, there is no one right way to go about forming them. However, the issues that we should like to address in establishing groups of this kind are:

- providing an umbrella of support
- securing freely chosen entry for participants
- gaining line manager involvement as appropriate
- sorting an initial agenda
- facilitating a start-up event
- ensuring conflicts are resolved
- dealing with productivity issues
- enhancing learning to learn
- disengagement

We will now address each of these in turn. Later in the chapter we offer some ideas towards the development of the skills we think you will find useful in doing these things.

Providing an umbrella of support

Under this heading we will look at:

- using steering groups
- using external facilitators (for readers inside companies)
- building a client system (for readers who are externals)
- tying into broad organizational goals

Using steering groups

In one organization where we were working we had been invited to facilitate a number of self-managed groups simultaneously, and we decided to propose the formation of a steering group to monitor the project. When this group first met, neither ourselves as contractors, nor the internal sponsors, nor the senior managers invited to join had a clear vision of the purpose or mode of operation of the group. Nonetheless, as time went on, it performed a number of crucial functions for the continuing success of the project. These included:

- providing the organization with a forum to raise reservations and concerns about the operations or goals of the project that could pass beyond rumour and innuendo to a mutually satisfactory resolution;

- giving the programme a power base from which to ask things of participants' line managers or human resource development coordinators in departments;
- being a sponsor and forum for discussion of evaluation studies of the project;
- acting as a sounding board for developments in the project—for example, at one stage, we proposed a special group for part-time managers in the organization with the slogan 'Part-timers have careers too'. We may not have progressed beyond the sloganizing had the steering group not encouraged us to research the issue further and then enthusiastically endorsed our proposal;
- acting as champion of the model of learning and the programme itself when the time came to merge it into a wider process of development within the organization.

We were fortunate in having as chair a senior manager whose unit had sponsored a great many people onto the initial tranche of the programme. He was not initially a devotee of self-development, but as time went on he became one, and served as an important link between the internal and external people running the scheme and the top management of the organization. His very neutrality was a great asset in dealing with the storms (teacup-sized and larger) that assail self-development initiatives.

Activity 4.3   Planning a steering group

For a self-development group you run or plan to run:

- Identify some purposes that a steering group might serve.
- Ask other parties to generate their own lists.
- Convene a meeting to pool ideas and to test out whether these advantages outweigh any disadvantages that people might come up with.
- If you decide to go ahead, prepare a short document outlining purposes, processes and membership.
- Make it happen.

Using external facilitators   The skills of running self-development groups, while clear and specifiable, are not very widely distributed in organizations. If you are in an organization and considering whether you need outside support, Activity 4.4 might help you decide.

Activity 4.4   Using outsiders: Trojan horse or lifeline?

Below are two lists, one suggesting advantages, one disadvantages of using outside support. Both lists are left incomplete for you to add your own ideas. When you've done this, complete List C, which asks you to review the items on the list for the option you reject and to work out ways to transform or overcome each item on that list.

List A   Outsiders as Trojan horses

- Outsiders will do the interesting work so our people won't develop these skills.

- Our department won't get the prestige associated with the project.
- They will cost the earth and jeopardize our other projects.
- They won't know enough about the organization's culture and will put participants off.
-
-
-
-

List B   Outsiders as lifelines

- Using outsiders provides an opportunity to develop the skills of our own staff.
- Their prestige will enhance the standing of the project.
- The cost of facilitation can be quickly adjusted in line with fluctuations in demand.
- They will provide a refreshingly dispassionate outside view on how we operate.
-
-
-
-

At this point, decide whether the balance of advantage lies in using outsiders or going it alone. Then, if you decide to bring them in, work through your List A, and write down ways of transforming or overcoming each item. Note these ideas in List C. Similarly, if you decide not to use outsiders, use List C to note ways of eliminating the down-side of the items in List B.

List C   Transforming threats into opportunities

-
-
-
-
-
-
-

Building a client system

Although this area is of crucial concern to those of us who act as external facilitators, it is also very important for internals as well.

Example   **Who am I working for?**

One of the most successful self-development groups that we have been associated with was run in an organization where one of us had been invited in by a senior manager who had engaged the commitment of her chief, and fixed up for an able and enthusiastic internal consultant to work on the project too. The programme was scheduled to run for a year, and as time went on the focus became narrowed down more and more onto the group itself. Everything was going well, there seemed to be plenty of wider support, so, nothing to worry about . . .

However, just as the end of the programme drew near, the initial sponsor, who had responsibility for human resource development issues, was moved onto other work which meant spending much of her time abroad. Her replacement had never heard of self-development before taking this role, and what he heard then he did not like. The chief retired, and the internal facilitator left to become a consultant. The participants, although enthusiastic, were relatively junior, and were also administrators in a professional organization, so lacked clout, to put it mildly. Client system? It went thataway!

Result: loads of satisfaction—no follow-on action.

Activity 4.5 *Doubling your client network*

For any current self-development project, draw a diagram of your client network. The one in the example above would have looked like this:

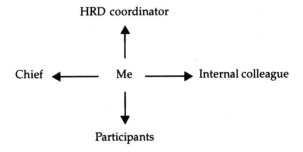

Now draw your own below:

Next, work out who could usefully be added to double the number of potential clients. If that still does not seem enough, add a few more. Then work out a way of drawing each of the new client groups into the project. List these below, and plan what is going to be done, by whom and when:

New clients	How draw in	Whose action	By when

Tying into broad organizational goals

The aims of individual members of self-development groups are often very diverse. However, overall, these groups tend to achieve a number of broad goals for members. Some of these are listed in Figure 4.2.

- Members work on problems and opportunities particular to their situation.
- Members develop skills in supporting and challenging others.
- Members increase their risk-taking skills.
- Learning and work are integrated.
- Members enhance their ability to review their own progress.
- Members learn how to learn and become more self-starting.
- Members become better at prioritizing and focusing on key issues.
- Learning is often shared with others.
- Members develop capability in managing change, in contributing to meetings and in developing their own people.
- Members are better able to integrate their home and work lives.

Adapted from Alan Mossman and Rory Stewart's 'Self-managed learning in organizations' Chapter 3 of Pedler, Burgoyne and Boydell 1988.

Figure 4.2 *Benefits of self-development groups*

The next activity asks you to link any organizational or human resource development goal that your organization may have to the benefits of self-development that you have discovered, and then to take advantage of these links.

Activity 4.6   Going for goals

- Through discussion or by reading published material, identify as many current overall goals for the organization as you can. Look out particularly for process goals—how power-holders in the organization want the place to be run in the future.
- Identify from your own experience and/or from the literature on self-development (Figure 4.2 above would get you started—Chapter 6 should keep you going for a week) the goals that your proposed self-development programme will achieve.
- Identify the overlaps between the two lists.
- Find out who are the champions of the organizational goals that your programme will support.
- Make sure they know about your programme and how it ties in to their goals.

The activities listed above will go a long way towards providing an umbrella of support. In addition, keep the aim of providing support as a goal in the forefront of your mind and stay alert to the possibility of finding other ways of achieving it.

Securing freely chosen entry for participants

However much participants have been nudged to apply for your programme, always make sure that they make the final commitment themselves. As a minimum, they could fill out an application form that invites them to specify why they want to be on the programme and what they want to gain from it.

In this section we suggest three ideas that can take the process of choosing to enter the programme usefully beyond the minimum. These are:

- spell out the commitment
- a taster event
- discussion with a previous participant

Spell out the commitment   If you produce a manual, or an initial diagnostic workbook, make sure that it specifies both the means of working and the amount of time—work and personal (if any)—that the programme is likely to take. Ask potential participants to discuss these sections with their line manager and, if possible, arrange for the three of you to meet to check out that it is this sort of programme, at this time, that is required.

A taster event   One of the best ways of testing out commitment and readiness is to run a 'taster event' of about half a day for potential participants. This is also an excellent forum for advertising and drawing potential members to the group. In the session it is useful to include some or all of the following components:

- outline of time commitment and process
- opportunity for some individual work identifying goals—possibly using questionnaires like those in Pedler, Burgoyne and Boydell (1986)
- work in pairs or small groups sharing this information
- a brief planning activity

An event like this will not only provide information, but will also give that all-important feel for the process.

Contact with previous participants   This contact can be given at the taster event, or phone number of willing volunteers from previous programmes (if any) can be given to aspirant members. This process needs handling with a little care—and perhaps two main pitfalls could usefully be pointed out to volunteer previous participants. These are:

- not to go overboard with enthusiasm, which may sound unduly evangelistic to the unenlightened. It is useful to be as explicit and concrete as possible, rather than emphasizing the intangible mystery of the process;
- not to reduce the process merely to handy tips—volunteers can be most helpful if they recognize that each group can maximize learning by, at least to some extent, finding their own path.

Some self-development programmes have used previous participants as off-line mentors for new members. If this is the case with your programme, then the previous members could explain how they see this working.

Gaining line manager commitment as appropriate   The title of this section includes the phrase 'as appropriate' because the amount of involvement of line managers in self-development programmes can vary enormously. Sometimes participants would like them to be heavily engaged, and the organization's human resource development structure reinforces this. On other occasions, the programme can be seen almost as an opportunity to develop *in spite of* the boss. In either event this relationship needs managing, and on one occasion we have held separate meetings with the line managers to keep them informed of the programme, as the participants did not want to engage with them at all. This was an extreme case, and our general principle is to involve the line managers to the maximum considered helpful by participants.

Example **Involving line managers in self-development**

In one of our major programmes of self-development we involved the line managers as follows:

- Manager and participant had a preliminary meeting where they discussed the participant's self-diagnosis against a questionnaire prepared specifically for the programme.
- They met a facilitator in a three-cornered discussion to clarify the nature of the programme, to enlarge the range of possible areas of learning on the programme if manager and participant had stuck unduly literally to the questionnaire, and to agree roles—particularly the role of the manager.
- A half-day, mid-programme workshop for line managers and participants was run to review how managers were getting involved and to share ideas. On occasions this workshop has been run just for the managers.
- *Ad hoc* meetings with manager/participant pairs and facilitators were held to discuss progress; these were also fixed if a participant acquired a new manager during the course of the programme.
- Final day involvement. The final day was invariably planned by participants, so the nature of the meeting with managers varied enormously. However, in almost all cases, managers were invited for part, not all, of the day, and the issues addressed included:
  —what we have learned
  —a review of the manager's role
  —how the relationship can develop from here

A dynamic which seems to be important to us, and which requires managing on self-development programmes involving line managers, is the issue of the ownership of the goals and the learning contract or agreement (see the discussion of skills for self-development, later in this chapter). In many organization cultures there will be a predisposition for line managers to take over the ownership and setting of the learning goals. It is part of the facilitator's role to keep this process firmly in the hands of the participant. It may be necessary to outline to managers the essential motivational and learning benefits of leaving the responsibility there.

Sorting the initial agenda

There are many means of establishing an initial agenda, and your preference among them may be influenced by the amount of chaos and ambiguity you can handle. It is also a good idea to recognize the amount of chaos the participants can take.

Figure 4.3 below, lists the means of arriving at an initial agenda, in approximate order of freedom of choice (starting from least choice), which also corresponds to the order of demand on tolerance of ambiguity of those involved.

---

1 Send a list of possible *activities* to participants, asking them to choose or rank order the items and return them to the facilitator.
2 Send a list of possible *needs* to participants, asking them to rank these and return them.
3 Have participants meet together and explore the possible activities from (1) above, and determine their own programme.
4 As (3), but with the needs from (2) above.
5 Have participants meet and offer them a range of self-diagnostic instruments to complete, then ask them to use the data from these to plan the programme.
6 When participants meet, say 'One task we have is to plan what we are going to do with the time available to us; I suggest that we do this now'.
7 At the first meeting, ask the group 'How shall we get started?'
8 At the first meeting sit in silence, and make only process comments on what is going on.
9 ⎫
10 ⎬   Add your own ideas.
11 ⎭

Figure 4.3 *Agenda-setting interventions*

You can use Figure 4.3 to explore your own style of agenda setting. We suggest a method in Activity 4.7.

Activity 4.7   *How do you set your agendas?*

• Choose from Figure 4.3 three possible styles of agenda setting.
• For each of your chosen styles, make notes under the following headings in the table below.

Possible style	Benefits for participants	Benefits for me	Difficulties for me	How to overcome difficulty
1				
2				
3				

- Having assembled this information, review your preferred style of setting agendas; decide whether you want to change it in some way, and whether there are any development needs that you have in order to make this change.

Facilitating a start-up event

Many self-development programmes get off to a solid start with a two or three day start-up event. The purposes of these events are often complex and overlapping. These purposes can include:

1 Introducing the idea of self-development
2 Carrying out individual diagnoses, preparing individual learning contracts and doing some individual planning
3 Doing (2) for the group
4 Developing individual learning skills
5 Building a learning group
6 Giving information about what can be learned and how
7 Seeking ideas for individual and group learning

Activity 4.8 encourages you to think about how you will balance a start-up event to help the group achieve the objectives that will be important in your context.

Activity 4.8   *Starting in balance*

Here is a list of dichotomies that may need balancing in your start-up event. If you have facilitated such an event before, mark where you came to rest on each of the dichotomies last time. Then look through the list again, and ask 'How could I alter the balance to maximize movement towards self-determination without overwhelming participants' toleration of ambiguity?' If you have not been involved in a start-up before, decide on where you want the balance to fall. Then, in either case, go about designing the event, bearing in mind the dichotomies. When you have finished your design, check it against the list, and adapt as necessary.

Dichotomies

Teaching	Exploring
Content	Framework
Knowledge	Skills
Forming group	Meeting needs of individuals
Own needs	Others' needs

Our own preferred position would be somewhat to the right in the first three dichotomies and near the centre in the last two that we listed. However, there will be particular programmes where a different balance is required, and by this stage in the book we do not expect you to be surprised to hear that *it all depends*, and that the important point for us is to bring these issues into awareness, and to recognize the possibility for free, informed choice.

**Ensuring conflicts
are resolved**

At this stage we will examine the types of conflict that can occur in self-development groups, and the general stance that we, as facilitators, take. In a later section of this chapter, on skills for self-development, we will return to the question of 'how to address conflict'.

At this stage we want to say three things:

1 Conflict is a natural part of group life.
2 Conflict is best addressed, not ignored.
3 Conflict is not always what it seems.

Conflict is a natural part of group life.   Tuckman, in his perceptive and rhyming summary of the research on group development, says that groups go through the following four stages:

• forming
• storming
• norming, and
• performing

One of the chief difficulties for groups in dealing with conflict is the catastrophic fears that it invokes ('If we look at this stuff then everything will fall apart'). So holding onto the position that conflict is a natural and inevitable part of group life, and that it can be handled more or less well, can be enormously helpful. When all else fails, remember the advice on the cover of *The hitch-hiker's guide to the galaxy*—DON'T PANIC.

Conflict is best addressed, not ignored.   We suggest that conflict is best dealt with because, if ignored, it can fester; but also because dealing with conflict can be such a rich source of learning.

Conflict can arise:

• between members of the group
• between a pair in the group
• between group members and yourself
• between the group and other parts of their organization

In all cases our role is to encourage and to enable members to deal with the conflict for themselves. They may be tempted to ascribe blame to the other party in the conflict, so one of the first things we may have to do is to help them get out of 'the blame frame'. While in a cast of mind that wants to blame, there is, of course, little chance of resolving the conflict, but also there is less chance of *learning* from the situation. The 'I'm responsible for everything' exercise, later in the chapter, may help here.

Conflict is not always what it seems.   The psychological process of projection is a pervasive feature of life. If a group is having difficulty sorting out its own way of working, members may be tempted to say 'Management hasn't got its act together about what they want from this programme'. If they are feeling angry with you for not telling them what to do, they may say 'You seem angry with us'. Projection happens when the projector is unhappy about some feelings vaguely sensed inside themselves, so they ascribe the feeling to someone else. Learning comes when the feeling is re-owned, expressed as something coming from them, and dealt with.

Dealing with productivity issues

In our experience, self-development groups differ in almost every conceivable respect *except* that at some stage in the life of every group someone will ask 'How does our group compare with other groups you've worked with?' A temptation at this point is to give the group detailed feedback on ways in which it is better than or falls short of memorable groups from your past. We think that this is a temptation worth resisting. If you give members what they ask, you are, first, taking evaluation out of their hands into yours and, second, moving into a ranking mode, of good and bad, better and worse. As Deming, the grand-daddy of Total Quality Management, says of this process 'It crushes you, crushes you'. So when this inevitable question comes up we tend to refer the group back to their own goals and invite them to review progress against these.

A second common request on this theme is 'Can you give us your feedback on how each of us is doing?' On the face of it, this can seem a more reasonable request than the first, and you may be tempted to give participants what they say they want. On the other hand, to do so may be to fall into the same trap we outlined above—of taking evaluation out of members' own hands. A response to this question that we often use is: 'Here are some criteria, which we discussed, for success in a group like this. Why not spend a bit of time reviewing your own progress against these? Then get into pairs and get some feedback from others or, if you prefer, do that in the whole group. If there is anything that I can add I'll do it then.'

Enhancing learning to learn

Alan Mumford, in Chapter 2 of Pedler, Burgoyne and Boydell (1988), suggests that learning to learn involves:

- knowing the stages of and blockages to learning
- understanding one's own preferred approach to learning
- using preferences, building new strengths and overcoming blockages
- applying learning back at work

This is an area where we can take the initiative in the life of the group, as members may have little experience in the area or, indeed, they may see little need for work on learning to learn. For example, in an activist culture, encouraging reflection can become a major theme in our interventions. One of our colleagues was working in such an organization, and was told after working with a group for some months: 'If you mention the need for reflection once more, someone's going to hit you, or think about doing so, anyway.'

Questions that address Mumford's four points, listed above, will therefore be a unique and valid contribution to the life of the group; and after a time you can encourage group members to pick up this orientation for themselves.

Disengagement   Towards the end of the life of a group, there are a number of processes that need to be handled. Often group members will deal with these with great skill. It can be useful to develop a mental list of these issues so that you can intervene if they are not being addressed. Activity 4.9 provides a framework for doing this.

Activity 4.9   Rules for disengagement

1 Think back over groups that you have been a member of that have ended well. What were the features that contributed to a good ending? List them:

-
-
-
-
-
-
-

When we did a similar exercise we came up with the following points:

- reviewed triumphs and disasters of the group
- laughed a lot
- forgave ourselves and each other for things done and not done
- committed ourselves to continuing contact and specified when, where and what
- restated initial affirmations, and reviewed how they felt now
- noticed all the unplanned ways we had developed as well as the ways we said we would
- celebrated small wins
- acknowledged the sadness of parting

2 Add any further thoughts to your list that may have been triggered by reading ours.
3 Carry your list in your mind in the last meetings of your group.

In addition to these points about the processes of the group, you may also want to consider various structural activities that may help to support participant re-entry or sustain the self-development initiative within the organization. These might include:

- Involving line managers in part of the final meeting.
- Inviting a member of senior management to talk about the organization's strategic direction, and to explore how self-development can contribute to this.
- Arranging for participants to offer mentoring services to subsequent group members.
- Formally planning continuing learning events or review meetings.
- Agreeing to write a biography of the group for publication in the house magazine.

It is a time, too, for acknowledging your own sense of loss if you will lose contact with the group.

Skills for the group facilitator

We now turn from our consideration of the three types of group to explore how facilitators can develop their skills in working with each kind of group. We list the skills for facilitating team building and action learning sets and then offer discussion and activities which can enhance your competence in each area. The final section of the chapter looks at the core skill in self-development groups—the art of 'making space'.

Skills for team building

There are many guides to team-building skills (such as Woodcock 1989). We are not trying to cover the whole range of skills that these sources address. Instead, we focus on specific activities that we have found crucial in turning the process of the group being *directed* by us into a process of their *finding their own direction*.

The skills we explore are:

- building environmental support
- building team vision
- modelling team dynamics
- addressing corrosive relationships
- putting gender on the agenda.

Building environmental support

When team building works well it draws the members closer together. An unintended consequence of this closeness can be that relationships to the environment of the team actually become more distant. For this reason, a direction that we can offer teams is to look out to their customers and suppliers. These relationships can go beyond the superficial pleasantness of customer care and preferred supplier status, to something rather deeper. Useful sources for exploring these issues are—for *customer relations*—Roger Harrison's challenging and beautiful AMED Focus Paper *Organisation culture and quality of service: a strategy for releasing love in the workplace* (1987), and for *supplier relations*—John Carlisle and Bob Parker's *Beyond negotiation: redeeming customer–supplier relationships* (1990). Activity 4.10 encourages you to explore some of these questions.

Activity 4.10   What do customers and suppliers want?

Step 1   Brainstorm two lists—one of suppliers and one of customers. If there are lots of individual ones, list categories rather than specific examples (e.g. raw material suppliers, corporate customers). Remember internal as well as external links.

Step 2   Invite the team to identify as many things as they can, which they think each of these customers and suppliers wants.

Step 3   Encourage them to make enquiries of actual customers and suppliers. A useful question might be 'What changes could improve the way we work/do business together?'

Step 4   Explore some of the questions raised by the sources cited above. For example:

- Do you feel treated as worthwhile individuals?
- Are your opinions about what you want and need respected?

- Are you treated on a level of equality?
- Do you experience caring and kindness in your relations with us?

Step 5   Check the responses to Steps 2, 3 and 4, and plan how you want to respond to them.

Building team vision

A temptation for the leader, fired up by the literature of excellence (e.g. Tom Peters' *Thriving on chaos* 1987) is to set an inspiring vision for her team and to sell it to them. A messier, slower and, in our experience, more lasting and impactful process is to encourage the team to develop their own. If you offer this direction to a team, then a particular skill you may require is in getting contributions from all members heard. Many teams suffer from premature closure in their decision making, and the use of brainstorming or rounds, where each member has the option of commenting and it's okay to pass, can contribute to a fuller exploration of options.

Modelling team dynamics

One approach that we have developed for exploring what is going on in a team (in members' own terms) is to encourage members to demonstrate what they see happening at work by building and explaining a model of the team. This does not necessarily require any advance preparation of materials. The bits and pieces in a hotel conference room often provide a rich source of symbols. In one team we worked with, 'lying in the mint jar' became a widely used term to describe managers retreating from the uncomfortable realities of everyday life. 'Lying in the mint jar with the lid on' was more serious as it prevented the manager (a balloon water glass in the modelling exercise) from hearing when it was going home time. Activity 4.11 offers a way of exploring team dynamics using modelling that requires just a little bit of preparation.

Activity 4.11   Russian dolls

A powerful set of objects for team members to project their views onto are the wooden Russian dolls that are widely sold in gift shops, and stack one inside the other. The traditional set has a woman figure, with impassive features and peasant clothes depicted on each doll. If you use these, then you can suggest that members present team dynamics in terms of, among others, the following aspects:

- Who is big, who small?
- Who is close to whom?
- Which way are they looking?
- Are they standing up or lying down; whole or truncated?
- Is anyone pointed one way from feet up, and another way from head down?
- Is anyone inside anyone else?

You can then explore movement and what characters say to each other.

Another elaboration is to have more than one set of dolls. We have found and used bandits and clowns and pipe-smokers, who add to the richness of initial images on which team members can build.

Viv Whitaker, an organization development consultant who first introduced us to this method of working, sometimes also uses an old set of wooden building blocks, which provide platforms and sanctuaries, and, perhaps most often in her experience, *walls* dividing one part of the team or its environment from the rest.

Sometimes, to be helpful, you need to ensure that one individual has a chance to build their own story before others contribute. On other occasions, we have witnessed highly energetic and purposeful sharing of ideas and images by all members of a team.

We would like to add three points about the use of this exercise. First, a period of reflective review is crucial to build on the insights that the exercise can give. Second, the exercise can deepen the issues being addressed, and, if you are not ready to help the team make it safe to deal with what comes out, then the exercise should be used with caution. Third, and as a consequence of the first two points, it can take a considerable amount of time to work through, and this must be allowed for.

The great strength of the exercise from a self-development point of view is that it provides an open space where the team members can express their own issues.

Addressing corrosive relationships

In some of our work with teams we have been faced with the dilemma of a particularly hostile relationship between two team members getting in the way of the team's development. We have experienced this situation leading to a bind, where the quality of the relationship prevents the building of trust and strength within the group to deal with the sour relationship. In such cases, we have occasionally worked with the two individuals concerned separate from the rest of the group. This is always a second best, in terms of enhancing self-development, but from time to time may provide the team with a start on which they can build. The example below gives an illustration of this process in action.

Example **Alexander and William**

Alexander is a chief officer in a large local authority department. William is his deputy. Four years ago, when Alexander was appointed from outside the organization, William had applied for the job, and had been disappointed not to get it. They are temperamentally at odds, Alexander preferring an informal style, and William valuing the frameworks and rules of public sector administration. Alexander is keen to establish a wide reputation for the department and sits on many national bodies. This increases the workload on an already hard-pressed administrative staff, who are managed by William and complain to him of Alexander's peremptory demands for adminstrative support for his personal projects.

William is a fierce fighter and bargains hard against the other direct reports of the Chief over budget and other issues. Team working is poor and staff of the department are heard to say 'When are the management team going to get their heads together, and stop fighting like kids?' However, the two protagonists exercise such a powerful influence on the other five team members that none of these feels able to confront the issue. When we mentioned the quality of work relationships there was a lot of denial of any problems. In team-building meetings William seems to be only half attending, and reads work documents not related to the task.

He meets one of us, and says that he cannot devote any more time to the team building, and adds that there is no point, because Alexander will not change and does not even want to. This last remark is taken as a starting point for a discussion, which leads to one of us offering to work with the two managers separate from the rest of the group.

When this three-cornered discussion takes place, William is able to voice a long stream of grievances both personal and organizational, and Alexander is able to acknowledge them. Alexander tells him that William's dogged style has made it difficult for Alexander to bring out the contributions of others in the team, and each acknowledges his apprehension in dealing with the other, and the isolation he feels in what could be a supportive team. They recognize each other's strengths and make a commitment to meet certain obligations, and to support each other in the process.

In subsequent team-building events William offers his full attention, and Alexander explores the impact of his style and his concern for external issues on other members. The other team members are now able to add their views and needs to the debate.

The example above illustrates a process of reconciliation sometimes referred to as the 'total truth process'. This model suggests that, if conflicts are to be resolved, then protagonists need to go through a sequence of feelings that may include:

- anger
- hurt
- fear
- doubt
- remorse
- 'I want'
- forgiveness
- appreciation
- love

In many cases, getting through this sequence in even the most favourable circumstances will be pretty daunting; in the example cited above, it was too much for the team to contemplate but, once started, was something they could build upon.

Putting gender on the agenda

Like other inequality issues, gender stereotyping is sometimes pervasive and, for insiders, hard to recognize. In teams it often rotates around simple rituals of men in the team playing sport together or going off to the pub without inviting women members. This can serve to exclude the women from important opportunities for informal information sharing and networking.

In such situations, the facilitator can have the role of bringing the issue into awareness. Giving this amount of direction can be useful, as team members may not be able to initiate discussion of the issue without being seen as engaging in special pleading, or being a spoilsport. In the cause of self-development, it seems to us important that we do not push our own agendas, regardless of the interests of the group. Nonetheless, raising an issue and inviting others to explore their perceptions of it may be a necessary opening.

Skills with action learning sets

There are a number of challenges facing members of an action learning set, and in this section we focus on skills that you can use to guide people facing these challenges. The challenges are:

- the challenge of not being taught
- the challenge of linking learning and work
- the challenge of learning from peers
- the challenge of learning over an extensive period, sometimes with long gaps between face-to-face contact sessions
- the challenge of reflecting in order to make sense of experience

The skills which help to meet these challenges we have called:

- Helping to cope with the loss of teacher
- Linking learning and work
- Learning from peers
- Keeping going
- Reflecting

We address each of these in turn.

Helping to cope with the loss of teacher

For many participants membership of an action learning set is a strange experience. They see themselves as sitting in a room with a handful of other learners and a teacher; and the teacher won't teach them anything! If they were sitting in a pub and there were no teacher present, then they may be saying to each other that teachers are useless, and they don't understand the situation. But, somehow, when there is a teacher on tap, it is tempting to put them on top as well.

Some of the ways we can help in this situation include:

- Giving a brief lecturette on the theory and practice of action learning (you could use the notes of Kath Aspinwall given earlier in this chapter, on page 81).
- Using our expertise and such authority as we have, to advocate the non-teaching strategy: 'Okay, if you say I'm an expert and you want my expert advice, then I advise you not to take my advice—but sort it out for yourself.'
- Offering a structure that will fill the aching void—the principal one in

an action learning set will be the equal sharing of time among members.

- Emphasizing our willingness to support the process, and our commitment to achieving excellent results. A lofty distance may be interpreted as a lack of interest or disdain at this stage, so—communicate cooperative intentions.
- Acknowledging the feelings of discomfort and encouraging the taking of first steps.

Later, we are more likely to be slowing things down and increasing reflection at the expense of hasty action, but at this stage our energy may be better focused on getting things going.

Linking learning to work

David Kolb (1985) describes the difficulty that managers often have of linking the processes of experimentation and experiencing (which are in the world of acting and doing) to the very different processes of reflecting and conceptualizing (which is the world of learning). We agree with Kolb that effective, experiential learning involves moving through both worlds sequentially to integrate the two.

One of the key elements in establishing the cycle in an action learning programme is the thoughtful choice of the projected action to be taken. If the project is too like ordinary work, it will not be seen as a source of rich learning. If it is too different from ordinary work, it may not be seen as relevant, although this will depend, in part, on the ability of the learner to conceptualize links between action learning and the rest of work. So, for example, in Revans' early work (1982) in Belgium, the participants worked in an unfamiliar function, and an unfamiliar industry. They were, however, a blisteringly bright bunch.

Other features of action learning activities that might highlight the possibility of learning include:

- having an interdepartmental focus in compartmental organizations;
- involving proactivity in organizations where participants typically do what they are told;
- involving contact with top management in hierarchical organizations, where such opportunities are rare;
- requiring contact with customers or suppliers where this is unusual behaviour for the people concerned.

Activity 4.12 invites you to think through your own criteria for action learning activities

Activity 4.12   Choosing an action

1 What are the criteria that come to mind for selecting projects? List them.

-
-
-
-

2 Check your objectives for the action learning programme and see if they suggest any additions to your list.

3 Explore with the stakeholders of the programme what they expect participants to get from it. See if their responses suggest further items.

4 Think through whether you want to set the projects for participants, or whether you can involve them more or less completely in setting the topic. Clearly, from a self-development point of view, the more they are involved the better. Encourage them to develop or add to the criteria for selection.

Learning from peers

We have talked about helping members not to expect to be taught, but there is another important aspect to using sets effectively, and that is enabling participants to learn from each other. Another wonderful Revans phrase is his description of set members as 'comrades in adversity'. How can these comrades support each other's learning, rather than become inward-looking and defensive? Revans argues that a key feature is the urgency and importance of the tasks (another criterion for Activity 4.12, perhaps?). However, there are certain things we as facilitators can do to encourage the process.

One activity that encourages learning from peers is the repeated seeking for needs and offers. At the start of an action learning programme, and also at times during the programme, we often ask people to write down what they want and what they have to offer, and we post the results for all to see. This process can lead to some one-to-one peer linkages of the kind: 'I see you need to know about project management. Well, I did a course on it before I took on a major project three years ago, and I'd be happy to talk it through with you.' It can also lead to offers of dialogue in the group, such as: 'If you want to talk through your problem of persuading the functional heads to take your task seriously, I'd like to do that in the group, because it will help me think through a different but related bit of persuading that I have to do.'

In fact, statements like the last one often take some time to emerge. A very hard thing for people to grasp seems to be the extraordinary and wonderful fact that if *I* am really 'selfish', and get into *my* difficulties and hopes, then this can be enriching and illuminating for others. Set members more often start by saying 'I don't want to hog the time: this can't be of any use to you'. Paradoxically, the more candid and the more specific they can be, the more use others appear to be able to make of the discussion for themselves. As set advisers we can serve a useful function in encouraging members to suspend disbelief until this process begins to happen.

Another thing we can do as set advisers is to notice the attention that members give to the contributions of their colleagues. We are not in the business of running a T-group, and process feedback in an action learning set is best justified in close and immediate relation to task performance. However, if we notice that members note down only things that *we* are saying and not ideas from peers, or if no one is summarizing what has been said, then it can be helpful to highlight this, and ask the group how its discussions could be made more productive.

Later in this chapter, under the heading 'Making space: core skills for self-development', we examine the key process of making space. The skills explored there are also highly relevant to the working of action learning sets.

Reflecting We said earlier in this section that, as the set develops, our role is likely to shift from energizing and speeding things up to reflecting and slowing things down. In many organizations managers get into a habit of almost frantic action. Some facilitators can get this way too. For optimum learning to take place, a more organic process, rather like breathing in and out, will help.

Breathing-out activities use up more energy than they generate. Examples include: brainstorming ideas; making plans for future action; struggling with difficult problems.

Breathing-in activities generate more energy than they use up. Instances of such energizing activities are: co-counselling pairs (where the helper's role is just to listen, not to suggest ideas); physical movement or relaxation; reviewing achievements.

One thing we can do as facilitators is to encourage our group to identify activities which for them are breathing-in or breathing-out, and to check how the balance is.

Another aid to reflection is Activity 4.13, where we explore how members can get into deepening their learning. We suggest that this activity works well because it is based on three principles:

1 It is helpful to see ourselves as the cause of what happens to us.
2 It is useful not to blame ourselves for these happenings.
3 We can enhance learning by generalizing from our experience.

The what-did-you-learn process described here is one that you can use with participants. We also find it helpful to employ on ourselves, so we have phrased this activity as a self-exploration process. It can be used to build on Activity 2.12 on page 35.

Activity 4.13 What did you learn?

1 Seeing ourselves as the cause

Think of an occasion where you have tried to get someone to help you, something has gone wrong, and you are inclined to ascribe this to the other person. For instance, you may have asked someone in Accounts for some information, and they have failed to deliver. At this stage, if asked what you have learned, you may reply:

> *'I'll never ask him to help me out again.'*

While this is a kind of learning, it is a rather negative and limiting sort. It certainly does not represent the development of any new competence on your part. So, just as an exercise, not necessarily because you believe it to be the case, imagine that the outcome was entirely your responsibility. With our example, we changed the statement to:

'I approached him the wrong way.'

How would you change yours?

2 Beyond the blame frame

If we are blamed, even if it is by ourselves, we can become defensive, and, as we suggested earlier in the chapter, it is useful to step out of the blame frame. As someone said, there is no such thing as a mistake, only an outcome ('I made another almighty outcome again yesterday'). Change your statement to take it out of the blame frame if it is in it. We changed our statement to:

'I approached him without thinking through the perspective he would take as an accountant.'

3 Generalizing

Our last statement only helps us in future dealings with the accountant. This is useful, but can we take the learning beyond this point so that it can help in relating to others? If your statement is still rather specific, see if you can widen its application somewhat. When we did this with ours, it became:

'I will approach people I need help from bearing in mind their needs and the pay-offs they might get from my proposal.'

The what-did-you-learn process, used judiciously, can help set members to derive meaning and value from set meetings, whether or not their own task is the topic of conversation. If taken one stage further—to explore the question 'What principles or theories does this last statement connect to?'—the process is also of use for learners preparing portfolios of learning for competency-based programmes and the accreditation of prior learning.

Keeping going   The final skill we will touch upon is not about speeding up or slowing down, but about keeping going. An action learning programme, like the clematis, is susceptible to sudden and unpredictable wilting. Energy can flow away and a sense of hopelessness invade the set.

As facilitators we can be sensitive to these changes of mood. It is often helpful simply to reflect what we see, rather than trying to recharge the group. Often, if the group becomes aware of what is happening to its energy, it will be able to identify the causes and come up with suitable remedies. Again, making space for this to happen can be our key contribution.

Additionally, there are structural interventions we can make to help members to keep going. Especially if the gap between set meetings is at the limit of the range we proposed at the start of this chapter (a month rather than a fortnight), it can be useful to do one or several of the following:

- establish a support network of phone calls to check out each other's progress;
- set up helping pairs where each keeps the other in mind and contacts them regularly;
- arrange an informal lunchtime meeting halfway between set meetings. This can be especially useful if most participants work at the same site and you are based somewhere else;
- at the end of each person's time in the set encourage them to establish a plan or target for what they aim to achieve before the next meeting.

You will be able to think of your own ideas relevant to your particular situation to add to our list. However, do not forget to ask the set to come up with their own suggestions, as this will create ownership and also give you further ideas to be creatively swiped and used elsewhere.

Making space: core skill for self-develoment

In this section we look at the essence of helping self-development to take place, which we believe to be the craft and art of making space. We do this using the analogy of architecture, and the example of Big Jim and the orgonauts.

Much of the work that architects do in the renovation and conversion of old buildings is concerned with making space. They create large open areas inside, removing dividing walls and even parts of floors, letting in light through larger windows, softening the inside/outside boundary further by bringing in lots of greenery, and so on.

Architecture means the thoughtful housing of the human spirit in the physical world.
William Meyer (1980) *Contemporary architects*, quoted by Knevitt p. 154

In organizational terms, one task of the moment is to clear space in oversupervised, overregulated regions in order to encourage members boldly to go where they have not gone before. Space making—creating gaps, breaks, openings, windows, elbow-room and so on—is also opportunity-making. Space making as a managerial task is a striking reversal of the bureaucrat's concern with space filling via job descriptions, key results areas, departmental boundaries and organization charts.

But space making is not simple or straightforward; it is not a task for modern Cromwells laying waste with ball and chain. Some of the old walls and floors need to remain for space to be put to use. Space in the unbounded sense—void, abyss, waste, infinity—is not likely to offer opportunities to those like us who have been brought up inside the confines of the bureaucratic form. Too much space and we will lose our sense of ourselves, lose our identities, and not be able to learn. We need time to learn to operate in these new spacious regions of the organization. Appropriate space and opportunity making is a sensitive and constructive art.

Despite the individualistic nature of this art there are some generalizations we can make. Table 4.2 gives examples of architectural devices together with possible organizational parallels:

Table 4.2 *Architectural/organizational parallels*

Architectural device	Organizational parallel
• removal of dividing walls	• demolishing departmental boundaries
• partial removal of floors	• removing levels of supervision
• outside staircases; putting service pipes, etc. outside	• hiving off service functions
• central courtyards, wells, atriums	• decentralized functions, central services removed
• added balconies	• encouraging outside trading
• recycled old materials	• retraining people, encouraging radical job changes
• historical objects used as sculpture	• celebrating differences, encouraging expression
• lots of inside greenery	• blurring home/work/community boundaries
• skylights in the roof	• opening up top management processes for inspection and comment
• larger windows	• encouraging outside secondments
• preserving historical objects	• bringing back selected retirees as part-time help—and not just top people

Table 4.2 applies the architectural metaphor to the whole organization. We can also study the art of space making at the level of a managers' self-development group. The analysis of 'Big Jim and the orgonauts' below reveals some ideas for space making at this level and perhaps provides clues for the manager as space maker on a grander scale. Many examples of space making can be found in the everyday practice of good managers everywhere, although perhaps they would not place those practices within this frame. The self-development group provides a particularly good case example because its primary purpose is to create space in which members may reclaim their sense of will (Pedler 1986, p. 20, Kemp 1989).

Example **Big Jim and the orgonauts**

Four members of a nine member self-development group in a large company had been meeting for five months. On this day they did a task that arose out of the air and is a good illustration of the making of space.

1 On the previous evening, in the bar, the foursome agreed to visit a fifth member's place of work, on the grounds that this would include him (although he had been unable to come to the meeting) and would be an interesting and useful afternoon. It also had the great advantage of filling in some time.

2 At 9.25 a.m. the next day, one of the two facilitators working with the group made the first move out of the coffee room. On reaching the workroom he remarked that the most difficult part of any action was getting out of your seat in the first place. One member said how tired he was, that he had only just noticed this and that he did not notice at work because he was always rushing about and never stopped. Another member said it was like going on holiday, you tended to collapse and it took a week to recover.

3 There followed 20 minutes or so of rambling discussion, then one member remarked that his back ached. Someone else said that this was often a sign of stress. These comments had been preceded by the familiar round of 'what shall we do next?' which had been inconclusive except that two members expressed a strong desire to do something active and get out and about.

4 After the backache discussion, the question of what to do next returned and it was suggested that the trainers should think up some tasks for the group to choose from. The trainers demurred somewhat, offering to go off and think up tasks as long as the group also devised some of their own. Before this could happen, someone suggested the idea of combining the afternoon visit with interviewing some people about stress—how they felt it and how they managed it.

[These elements, expressed here sequentially, were not planned and could not be predicted. As a way of deciding 'what to do next', they stand in stark contrast to rational planning processes. Here is evidence of opportunism, avoidance, risk taking, collaborative creativity and also, most importantly, of stochastic or random elements that contributed to the evolution of the task.]

The four members then got down to planning the task, designing a questionnaire, discussing their approach, sample size and so on. They called upon one of the trainers, who had previous experience in survey research, as a consultant from time to time. The trainer prompted on issues of confidentiality, on members' assumptions as to how they would be received and perceived and as to how this would influence the validity of their data, and so on. He also encouraged the group to specify learning objectives for the task and generally to look upon it consciously as a learning experiment and experience.

[At this point both members and trainers were in familiar roles and felt useful, purposeful and happy.]

During the afternoon, the four members, hosted by the fifth, interviewed some 25 members in the host organization and brought their data back for analysis. One member took responsibility for collating the data and producing a report, which in due course was circulated to those involved and other interested people.

On arriving back from their survey, the four managers relaxed and had a cup of tea. They were full of beans and very pleased with themselves. In the conversation that followed one of them wondered aloud how Jim (the 'big boss') handled his stress—he had the top job, so he must feel it most. One of the trainers suggested that they should take Jim up on his offer to 'go anywhere in the business and talk to anyone who wanted to talk to him'. After some consternation and discussion, and with great daring, one of the managers, accompanied by a friend, went off to telephone the Great Man. They came back elated. They had got through to Jim who had spoken to them and offered two dates.

In the self-development group the trainer's enabling role is very different from that of the instructor or director. Courses are unbroken flows of trainer-planned and trainer-directed activities, where the only spaces are for coffee and meals. In the self-development group a main aspect of the trainer's task is to create space in contrast to the busyness of managers' action-packed lives, and indeed in contrast to action-packed management courses. This space provides the opportunity for reflection, a chance to stop and think and feel that your back aches. Such reflection is generally acknowledged to be an essential part of the learning process, as we discussed earlier in this chapter when we were exploring skills for facilitating action learning sets.

But the precious space created by a self-development group is not just for reflection. Managers are primarily concerned with the study of action rather than of contemplation, however much the latter may be a useful part of the former. When the members of a self-development group, individually and collectively, are faced with the problem of emptiness—with the absence of syllabus, daily work agenda, or time structure—they are confronted with the problem of making use of the time that is suddenly and awkwardly at their disposal. They have to learn how to act in this setting and become acutely aware of the difficulty of taking that first step, of getting up from the chair, or proposing a task to their peers—things which, within the familiar structure of the manager's or trainer's role, they would have no difficulty in doing almost without thought. In attempting action in these circumstances we become especially aware of the effort of conscious action from the critical point before that faltering first step is taken . . . the step of being first to speak, and so on.

We are not usually exposed to such an extended study of the genesis of action. Yet action is the manager's *raison d'être*, and learning how to act in the unstructured, open spaces of the new, flexible learning organization is increasingly necessary. It's like learning to walk as an adult after an enforced period of immobility. Walking in space offers greater freedoms but requires new ambulatory skills. The art of space navigation in organizations we might call 'orgonautics', the managers who operate in the newly created opennesses—'orgonauts'.

Developing orgonauts

What can managers do to help their people function in space? In the renovated bureaucracy? How can we be helped to embrace the opportunities inherent in the new structure? If there are lessons to be drawn from the example of the self-development group, then perhaps the actions of the trainers in this setting are instructive.

From the experience of working with self-development groups, the following actions help to create space and encourage members to take their first faltering steps as orgonauts:

- stopping talking;
- not talking when expected to, especially when being asked 'What do we do next?' or any other question of a student-to-tutor nature;
- allowing silences to develop (silence = space); being as helpful as possible in making these silences safe for group members, e.g. by asking them to talk about how they felt during a silence;
- stopping teaching, inputs, directions—except where these are requested by members to assist in a self-set task, and only when the trainer is being used as *an* authority rather than being seduced into being *the* authority;
- slowing things down—people, discussions, processes; encouraging reflection at the expense of action 95 per cent of the time;
- questioning members' motives in leaping into the first action they think of;
- deepening as well as slowing discussions, sifting the minutiae to the surface and bringing the deeper structures and textures to light for observation and analysis;
- physically moving away from the focus, from the front of the room;
- leaving the room;
- encouraging people to act on their own initiative;
- daring members to question assumptions and act on the basis of new possibilities;
- joining with members from time to time in tasks and ceremonies.

And there are many others.

Beyond the face-to-face level of the small group, larger structural interventions are required to create the necessary space. Examples can be found of organizations that have scrapped detailed job descriptions, have taken steps to increase information flow and reduce secrecy and confidentiality, or have thrown away the fat rule book in favour of general principles. All such interventions can create space for orgonauts, although they are likely to be specific to particular organizations depending upon their historical development. We explore these issues in greater depth in the next chapter.

The general principle underlying the creation of organizations as opportunity structures is the concern to 'upsize the capacity of everyone'. This means creating the conditions in which people are empowered and encouraged towards self-direction, in the expectation that confidence stems from taking responsibility for our actions and doing it for ourselves. Anything that 'downsizes' or diminishes even one person, diminishes us all. The organizational architect is working not only to bring light and space into old bureaucratic forms, but is also working against the many ways we have of diminishing ourselves.

References

Carlisle, J. and R. Parker (1990) *Beyond Negotiation: Redeeming Customer–Supplier Relationships*, McGraw-Hill, Maidenhead.

Harrison, R. (1987) *Organisation Culture and Quality of Service: a strategy for releasing love in the workplace*, AMED, London.

Kemp, N. (1989) 'Self-development: practical issues for facilitators', *Journal of European Industrial Training*, 13(5), pp. 1–28.

Knevitt, C. (1985) *Space on Earth*, Thames TV International, London.

Kolb, D. (1985) *Experiential Learning*, Prentice-Hall, NY.

Larson, C. E. and M. J. LaFasto (1989) *Teamwork: what must go right/what can go wrong*, Sage, Newbury Park, Ca.

Leary, J. and M. Leary 'Transforming your career', Chapter 10 in Pedler, Burgoyne and Boydell (1988).

Mumford, A. 'Learning to learn and management self-development', Chapter 2 in Pedler, Burgoyne and Boydell (1988).

Pedler, K. (1986) 'Development within the organisation: experiences with management self-development groups', *Management and Education Development*, 17(1), pp. 5–21.

Pedler, M. (ed.) (1991) *Action Learning in Practice* (2nd ed.), Gower, Aldershot.

Pedler, M., J. Burgoyne and T. Boydell (1986) *A Manager's Guide to Self-development* (2nd ed.), McGraw-Hill, Maidenhead.

Pedler, M., J. Burgoyne and T. Boydell (1988) *Applying Self-development in Organizations*, Prentice-Hall, Hemel Hempstead.

Peters, M. (1987) *Thriving on Chaos*, Macmillan, London.

Revans, R. W. (1982) *The Origins and Growth of Action Learning*, Chartwell-Bratt, Bromley.

Revans, R. W. (1983) *ABC of Action Learning*, Chartwell-Bratt, London.

Woodcock, M. (1989) *Team Development Manual* (2nd ed.) Gower, Aldershot.

5 Working with the Learning Company

In Chapter 1 we summed up the developer's task in self-development as being that of empowering people to learn from acting, and to act on the basis of their learning. Throughout this book we have looked at the various settings in which we try to do this. Figure 5.1 shows again the developer's field of operations.

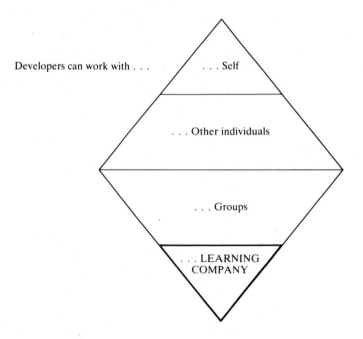

Developers can work with . . .

. . . Self

. . . Other individuals

. . . Groups

. . . LEARNING COMPANY

Figure 5.1   *Developer's diamond field*

In this chapter we deal with the bottom point of this diamond field—working with the organization as a whole. Rather like the 'self' field, this is a new focus for many developers who have tended to see themselves as dealing mainly with individuals and groups. We think this field is the new frontier for developers and that our craft has now come to the point where this challenge can be taken up. As a reminder, we use the word 'company' instead of the more usual 'organization', to embrace all groups or collectivities of people working in company on a task, and not to refer to any specific legal form. In this sense, a school or a hospital is just as much a company as a large commercial organization, indeed often more so. In this field, the developer's task is to do with creating an awareness and understanding of what working in company means, and how we, as companions, might accomplish our task better.

We think this is the new frontier, first because individual and group interventions are clearly not sufficient to create the flexibility and adaptability that companies are required to show in the face of various challenges. Indeed, it can be argued that the very success of some methods for *individual* and *team* development lead to the paradoxical experience of the *company*, its rules, regulations, management style etc., perceived as being restrictive, unimaginative and secure to the point of being a straitjacket. If we add to this the emerging view of organizations as organisms interacting ecologically with other organisms, rather than being seen as the complex machines that dominated thinking about organizations in the 1960s and 70s, then they are things that can learn rather than entities too complicated to mess about with. Machines can't learn, they are not living things, you might say, so what can I do that will possibly affect their mysterious ways? I am just a cog in a big wheel, I know my place and I do my bit (and, often, not a bit more). If, on the other hand, this is a living, learning thing, like me but different, where I can have some influence, then I am encouraged to think bigger, act more with the whole company in mind.

Before considering what a Learning Company might look like, complete the questionnaire in Activity 5.1.

Activity 5.1 *Measuring the quality of your learning climate*

For each of the following 10 dimensions ring the number, from 1 to 7, that you think best represents the quality of the learning climate in your company.

1 Physical environment—the amount and quality of space and privacy afforded to people; the temperature, noise, ventilation and comfort levels.

People are cramped with little privacy and poor conditions	1 2 3 4 5 6 7	People have plenty of space, privacy and good surroundings

2 Learning resources—numbers, quality and availability of training and development staff; also books, films, training packages, equipment, etc.

Very few or no trained people; poor resources and equipment	1 2 3 4 5 6 7	Many development people and lots of resources; very good facilities

3   Encouragement to learn—the extent to which people feel encouraged to have ideas, take risks, experiment and learn new ways of doing old tasks.

Little encouragement to learn; low expectations of people in terms of new skills and abilities	1 2 3 4 5 6 7	People are encouraged to learn at all times and to extend themselves and their knowledge

4   Communications—how open and free is the flow of information? Do people express ideas and opinions easily and openly?

Feelings kept to self; secretive; information is hoarded	1 2 3 4 5 6 7	People are usually ready to give their views and pass on information

5   Rewards—how much are people rewarded for effort? Is recognition given for good work or are people punished and blamed?

People are ignored but then blamed when things go wrong	1 2 3 4 5 6 7	People are recognized for good work and rewarded for effort and learning

6   Conformity—the extent to which people are expected to conform to rules, norms, regulations, policies rather than think for themselves.

Conformity to rules and standards at all times; no personal responsibility taken or given	1 2 3 4 5 6 7	People manage themselves and do their work as they see fit; great emphasis on taking personal responsibility

7   Value placed on ideas—how much are ideas, opinions and suggestions sought out, encouraged and valued?

People are 'not paid to think'; their ideas are not valued	1 2 3 4 5 6 7	Efforts are made to get people to put ideas forward; there is a view that the future rests on people's ideas

8   Practical help available—the extent to which people help each other, lend a hand, offer skills, knowledge or support.

People don't help each other; unwilling to pool or share resources	1 2 3 4 5 6 7	People very willing and helpful; pleasure is taken in the success of others

9   Warmth and support—how friendly are people in the company? Do they support, trust and like each other?

| Little warmth or support; this is a cold and isolating place | 1 2 3 4 5 6 7 | Warm and friendly place; people enjoy coming to work; good relationships = good work |

10 Standards—the emphasis placed on quality in all things; how far do people set challenging standards for themselves and each other?

| Low standards and quality; no one really cares | 1 2 3 4 5 6 7 | High standards; everyone cares and people pick each other up on work quality |

This learning climate questionnaire is adapted from Pedler and Boydell (1990) *Managing Yourself*, pp. 203–10.

Scoring

If your score comes to 30 or less, you're working in a poor learning climate. Learning Companies aspire to scores in the 50 to 70 range as the best guarantee of future survival, maintenance and development.

One of the defining characteristics of the Learning Company is being a place that encourages everyone who works in it or who has contact with it to learn. It has the 'learning habit' so that actions taken for reasons of production, marketing, problem solving or customer service also yield a harvest of reflections, insights and new ideas for action.

If you carry out a survey of the whole company, however, you may find differences of approach in the various parts of the organization. How do you explain this? The person in charge of a department usually has the biggest influence on the learning climate. Does that person have the development of an excellent learning climate as one of her key objectives?

We can see from this simple survey that whether people learn is due not only to their own efforts and the quality of the team they belong to, but also to the learning climate of the whole company. This is a quality of the whole and not just of parts. This capacity to learn is at the centre of an emerging model or aspiration for the company.

Learning Company defined

A Learning Company is . . .

. . . one which facilitates the learning of all of its members *and* continuously transforms itself as a whole.

(Pedler, Burgoyne and Boydell 1991, p.1)

Note the two aspects of this definition. A Learning Company not only has a good learning climate and encourages everybody to learn; it also seeks to create and maintain a collective self-learning capacity. It is this notion of the company as a whole organism which can be said to learn that poses the most compelling challenge of the moment.

It needs to be said here that, in one sense, there is no such thing as a Learning Company. We can't take you out and show you one. It is not even desirable to name this or that organization in this way. There are two reasons for this: first, to do so would imply that there is a single model or 'blueprint' to follow, and we don't believe this is the case. The second point is that giving any company this accolade would imply something finished. After Peters and Waterman (1982) identified a number of 'excellent' companies, both researchers and the markets spent the next few years proving they weren't so good. The Learning Company is beyond excellence in this sense—you do not arrive but the journey brings its own benefits.

The Learning Company is an idea or metaphor that can serve as a 'guiding star'. It can help people to think and act together on what such a notion would mean to them now and in the future. Like all visions, it can help to create the conditions in which some of the features of a Learning Company could be brought about. In Gergen's (1978) terms it is a 'generative theory', that is, one that mobilizes energy to shape shared perceptions and the will to change, as well as leading to concrete action. Such a theory encourages people to create their own vision in action and not to imitate that of others. For this reason we should resist calling any actual organization a 'Learning Company'. We can say that this company or that organization has certain Learning Company features, but that is as far as we would want to go.

Importance of the Learning Company concept

There are many reasons for adopting the theory of the Learning Company: fulfilling the potential of all our people individually and collectively; solving the pressing problems of the community, and so on. But, for the moment, let's take a 'bottom line' view. In some research we did we found that senior managers were excited by the idea of the Learning Company because it promised them competitive advantage— 'Just think what it would do for us in the market place' said one (Pedler, Burgoyne and Boydell 1988, p. 8).

In many organizations 'business strategy' means looking at what your competitors are doing and imitating them. In today's rapidly moving markets this is like photographing a moving car—by the time you have analysed and implemented the data the car is miles away. This is the game of 'catch up' and you never do. The essence of a good business strategy lies in creating tomorrow's new opportunities and advantages as well as continuing to deliver today's products and services, and doing this at a rate that is at least as fast as the rest of the market. In the words of a recent paper: 'An organisation's capacity to improve existing skills and to learn new ones is the most defensible competitive strategy of all' (Hamel and Prahalad 1989, p. 69).

There is a massive underdeveloped potential in most organizations. The ability to transform this potential in all aspects of company operations could result in extraordinary growth, great improvements in the quality of service or dramatic increases in morale and motivation. The desire for this sort of transformation could be central to business strategy. Most organizations are geared to incremental rather than transformational growth and change. For example, many companies measure success in one of three ways:

- against last year's performance
- against last year's budget
- against their competitors' performance

These comparisons are historical and generally do not look to the future. As habitual reflexes, they tend to perpetuate average perform-ance and to buttress the *status quo*. The right comparison is against what is possible. Current performance may look good against the average, but what could it be like? What is the potential that we could realize together? What is going on out there that we could work with? How can we work together differently?

These are the sort of questions asked in a Learning Company. The best way of keeping up with the business is seen to depend on enhancing the learning capacity of both individuals and the company as a whole. The need to adopt Learning Company strategies comes from environmental pressures without and also from people's natural striving towards personal development within. Pressures are increasing at the time of writing as a result of several factors; for example:

- the decline in the birth rate is reducing home markets and labour supply;
- internationalization of trade is creating European and global markets with exposure to increased competition, low-cost producers, and so on;
- managers are becoming better trained and more sophisticated.

For public sector and non-profit companies, times are also increasingly hard. They have felt some of the above pressures while also experiencing:

- increased demand for services with decreasing government funding;
- a severe crisis of confidence because of privatization and the under-valuing of the idea of 'public service';
- low morale due to staff cuts and relatively low earnings.

But the fundamental problem is the same as for those in the commercial world—how to let go of old ways of thinking and managing and embrace the new imperatives, while preserving and enhancing what is good and enduring. This means fundamental, not superficial, changes; what Argyris and Schon (1978) have called 'double loop' as opposed to 'single loop' learning. Single loop learning involves making small, incremental changes in existing systems and gradual improvements in efficiency. Double loop learning is about making major changes in values, assumptions, goals and operating procedures; in short, trans-forming the old to create a new company.

Characteristics

While shying away from a blueprint or model, our recent research suggests a number of characteristics that we might expect to find in any company that sets out to become a Learning Company. Developers may find themselves asking at this point: 'What's my role in all this? How can I get involved here?' It is difficult to be specific about the developer's role at the present time. We are in the early days of the quest for the Learning Company and various companies and people are engaged in pioneering their own approaches to achieve their visions. One of the needs of the time is to share what we call the various 'glimpses' of this vision, some of which can be found in *The Learning Company* (Pedler, Burgoyne and Boydell 1991).

Developers can make a useful start by collecting and disseminating these 'glimpses'. They can also encourage managers and other people to test the learning climate in their workplaces and to develop their own visions of what the Learning Company might look like for them. We will return to this theme later. Although we have said that there is no such thing as a blueprint of the Learning Company and that each company or organization must set about re-inventing the wheel of their own learning business, it is possible to assemble a sort of 'identikit' picture of the Learning Company from what various people are saying. Before going on to do this we return to a diagram we used in Chapter 1 and take it a bit further (see Figure 5.2). Again P = problem and S = the proposed solution.

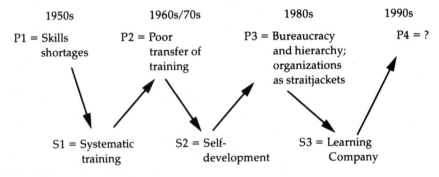

Figure 5.2 *An extended problem-solution map of training and development*

In Chapter 1 we got as far as self-development (S2) and this can be seen as leading to a perception of organizations as straitjackets, where empowered individuals find themselves increasingly frustrated and unable to realize their new-found skills and confidence. The company as a whole is too rigid and unadaptive. A Learning Company is one response to this problem.

Dimensions of a Learning Company

In seeking to become a Learning Company, any company could test itself against eleven dimensions (Pedler, Burgoyne and Boydell 1991).

1 Learning strategy	7 Enabling structures
2 Participative policy making	8 Boundary workers as environ-mental scanners
3 Informating	
4 Formative accounting	9 Intercompany learning
5 Internal exchange	10 Learning climate
6 Reward flexibility	11 Self-development for all

A **learning strategy** is not a right-first-time, 'Charge of the Light Brigade' approach, but one that allows business plans to be developed and for-mulated 'as we go along'. To do this, managerial acts should be seen as *experiments* and not as solutions. Deliberate small-scale experiments and feedback loops are built into plans so that they can be continuously improved in the light of experience.

In **participative policy making** the debate over company business goals is widely shared. All members have a chance to discuss and contribute to major policy decisions. There is a deliberate fostering and encourage-ment of creative contributions and a recognition that debate involves conflict between different positions and views. There is a belief that airing differences and working through conflicts is the way to reach business decisions to which all members are likely to be committed.

One way of structuring the debate so that different views are sought within a process that channels the conflict is described in the case below.

Learning from dialectic

Many managerial problems turn out to be messy and poorly defined. It is sometimes hard to tell the problem from the symptoms or to choose the relevant information from the vast amount available. Matters seem to be full of contradictions and paradoxes. There are different values among members, which lead to political and emotional clashes . . .

The stresses of managing ambiguous situations can be enormous. In such situations we are tempted to go for 'quick fixes' or to contain the conflict and confusion in some way—often for the sake of our own comfort or health. Learning Companies have to do better than this. Conflict is stressful but also a source of creativity, of testing old ideas and generating new ones. An organization that structures out conflict will also cut out challenge, risk, creativity and learning.

Here is one way, using three groups taken from the organization, to conduct a dialectic to try to get the benefits of conflict without the destruction.

1 Three groups, A, B and C, are set up to tackle an agreed problem area. The most senior person is put in Group C.
2 Group A goes off and develops an analysis and a plan for action on the problem, using any agreed method.
3 A's list of key assumptions is then turned over to Group B, which has the job of preparing counter-assumptions and an anti-thesis to A's plan.

4 Next, Group C facilitates a structured debate. A and B take turns to
   give spirited presentations, outlining their assumptions and the key
   data that they consider of importance. Each then probes the
   weaknesses in the other's plans, using wit and humour as well as
   logic and analysis. A sense of the dramatic is helpful here. The
   facilitator(s) must work to balance combativeness with goodwill, and
   prevent personal attacks. The rest of Group C note significant points
   and omissions.
5 Once the arguments begin to be repeated, the facilitator ends the
   debate and calls a break to allow members to socialize and re-connect
   at the personal level.
6 Then the whole conference, led by members of Group C, generates a
   list of agreed assumptions, a set of key data and a plan for action.

This approach can surface existing differences, tensions and values. The
clash of views can create something new—a third position from the
opposing two—which may possess aspects of both, together with higher
validity or acceptability than either. It is a good way to test a plan, and a
method for involving more people and more parts of the organization
in policy making.
Source: Michael McCaskey 1988

Informating describes that state of affairs where information technology
is used not just to automate, that is to take out the element of human
intelligence, but to inform and empower people to ask questions and
take decisions based on available data. Informating systems are designed
to provide members with access to all relevant information on the company in order to speed decision making. Information technology and
public domain databases give control to front line workers who can
'interrogate' these for information. Information systems are designed to
encourage learning and are interesting and even fun to use. The
description that follows illustrates how informating is changing the way
things are done.

Working in the electronic learning net

Computer Mediated Information Systems (CMIS) exploits the store,
processing and retrieval capabilities of the company mainframe for
internal and external communications. Databases, texts, articles, reports,
manuals and directories can be held for quick and easy access by members. Communications software, including EMail, Bulletin Boards and
Conferencing, allows for interaction between members, both person-to-
person and among dispersed groups. CMIS provides an electronic
learning environment where all members have equal access to data and
are able to communicate freely.

Any member can take part and all the company PCs are networked
through the mainframe with relevant external systems. Thus remote
access to national and international knowledge networks is available
within the company at any time. CMIS is increasingly being used to
deliver all kinds of education and training programmes in which users

typically report higher levels of interest, involvement and personal control than with conventional delivery methods. CMIS also provides for the distributed knowledge networks which are at the heart of up-to-date professional practice.

Helen McGuire works for a large international firm of consulting engineers as an internal management adviser. She is currently involved with a project team that is designing and building an integrated steel plant in the USSR.

As part of her work with the project team, Helen puts out regular progress reports of the project on the internal network Bulletin Board. On arriving at work on Monday she finds various EMail items from the weekend. One is from a manager in New Product Development asking for details of the project planning methods being used. Another is a request from an engineer for a short attachment for personal learning purposes with the project team. While printing these for presentation to the team later in the week, Helen sends an urgent request to Finance for clarification of a budgetary procedure being used on the steel project.

Helen also belongs to a professional association and has been taking part in an online seminar on new organizational structures. This morning she logs in to the seminar and finds that since she last took part several members have been exchanging ideas about 'temporary structures' and 'opportunity structures'. After scanning the summaries she downloads the full texts for later study. Meanwhile, she makes some notes and prepares some questions to add to the discussion section of the conference later on. She then logs in to the Papernet held by her association to see whether there are any items relevant to the steel plant project. She notes the names and numbers of two members offering papers on project management and cross-cultural issues. Finally, before going to a 10 a.m. meeting, she sends travel warrant requests and last month's expenses through to the relevant sections via EMail.

Returning some two hours later, Helen deals with a query about her travel requirements before logging-on again and instructing her PC to send the previously noted comments to the organizational structures conference and to send requests for the Papernet offerings. She has also received an invitation from Vienna to contribute to an electronic journal on 'Managing in a Unified Europe' which addresses comparisons and contrasts between western and eastern approaches. She makes notes in her computer diary to remind her to clear come papers on the USSR project with the project team before offering them to the journal.

Source: D. McConnell and V. Hodgson (1990) in Pedler, Burgoyne and Boydell (1991)

With **formative accounting and control** the essential control systems of accounting, budgeting and reporting are structured to assist learning from the consequences of managerial decisions. Systems promote managerial self-control by encouraging individuals and units to act as small businesses within a regulated environment. The emphasis is on auditing, controlling, and accounting for one's own actions.

Accounting roadshows at Mercian Windows

Following several requests after a series of Customer Care programmes, the finance department at Mercian Windows set up a roadshow to go at fairly short notice to any of the 38 branch offices of the company. As an operationally decentralized but financially centralized organization, Mercian Windows needed to ensure that branch management teams understood the way money worked in the company in order to make better business deals and, in particular, to take appropriate risks.

The roadshow consists of the branch accountant in Head Office, the factory accountant, the internal auditor and an attached management trainer. The roadshow includes a video, some short presentations, self-development activities designed to illustrate the workings of the money system, and opportunities for personal one-to-one or small group coaching to work through specific issues. In addition, following a roadshow visit, branch managers are encouraged to set up a further learning contract with Head Office which can involve further study, visits and contacts.

The accounting roadshow has certainly shown Head Office to be responsive and resulted in some branch managers being better informed. In the Learning Company we would ask a further question— has it resulted in any changes to the way finance is managed in the company? The finance director was cautious on this point—'It has certainly resulted in changes to the way we present financial information in the company' was as far as he would go.

Source: Pedler, Burgoyne and Boydell (1991)

Internal exchange involves all internal units and departments seeing themselves as customers and suppliers contracting with one another in a partly regulated market economy. Each department sets out to delight its customers and, through overall collaboration within the company, achieve optimum performance. Individuals, groups, departments and divisions exchange information on expectations and give feedback on goods or services received in order to improve the quality of relationships. Management facilitates and coordinates; control is achieved through negotiation and mutual adjustments between units.

Reward flexibility recognizes that, with increasing degrees of participation we need to explore alternative ways of rewarding people. The assumptions on which reward systems are based—why we pay people differentially; whether we use money to 'make' people work harder, and so on—are examined to discover the principles on which rewards are predicated. The aim is to reward people in terms of what they *need* as well as what they *offer*, and on the basis of commonly agreed principles. Non-monetary rewards may be especially important in providing choice for members.

This is perhaps the most difficult of the eleven dimensions on which to make progress since it probably involves not only the redistribution of reward, but also the redistribution of power. However, several of the other characteristics of the Learning Company also imply a redistribution of power from the 'top pyramid' to the wider company.

Enabling structure are those which create opportunities for individual and business development. Roles are loosely structured to allow for personal growth and experiment. Departmental and other boundaries are seen as temporary structures that can flex in response to environmental or other changes. The aim is to create an organizational architecture that gives space and headroom for growth now and in response to future challenges.

Boundary workers as environmental scanners is an activity carried out by all members who have contact with customers, clients and other stakeholders external to the organization. These boundary workers deliver goods and services *and* systematically collect and carry back information that is collated and disseminated. There are clear opportunities for customers, suppliers and stakeholders to raise questions, give feedback and make requests to the company.

Intercompany learning means engaging in a number of mutually advantageous learning activities. The Learning Company is always on the lookout for new possibilities with customers, clients and even competitors. The company shares information and collaborates with stakeholders on joint research and development activities. There is the ability at all levels within the organization to compete and collaborate as the need and opportunity arises.

We have already spoken about a good **learning climate** where managers see their primary task as facilitating members' experimentation and learning from successes and failures. It is normal to take time out to reflect on practice, and senior managers give a lead in questioning their own actions and in seeking to learn from experience. Mistakes are dealt with constructively, differences are recognized as the basis of new learning and central importance is attached to the idea of continuous improvement.

Self-development for all means that resources and facilities for self-development are available to all company members. People are encouraged to take responsibility for their own learning and development. No one is sent—although they may choose to go—on a course, but members report on their learning activities as a regular aspect of the appraisal process and discuss their further learning needs.

Becoming a Learning Company requires an overall effort to create, maintain and realize the vision. To illustrate just one aspect of this process, one key factor is the company's ability to challenge itself, to give itself that kick which can stimulate double loop learning through questioning of current operating norms and assumptions. Some companies try to build this in.

The management challenge

Challenging our own norms and assumptions is difficult. As their names imply, these everyday structures of individual and corporate lives are taken for granted and not noticed—in effect, are invisible to those who follow or hold them. They are much more obvious to others following different norms and assumptions, who, while similarly blind to their own 'taken-for-granteds', can ask penetrating and provoking questions of us.

Royal Dutch Shell have tried to incorporate this potentially valuable process into their company operations with what they call 'the management challenge'. Every three years a senior executive from another plant and usually another country visits a given location to deliver a challenge to management. He or she spends a week or so at the site, wandering around, reading reports, talking to people, before challenging the managing team. This involves presenting observations, impressions, making suggestions but, above all, asking 'naive' questions—questions that an insider would not ask because the answers are obvious. These questions are basically of the nature: 'Why do you do such and such?' or 'How does this and that contribute to plant efficiency?' The local managers must publish the challenge and their responses to it.

The management challenge is one way of ensuring that the 'hidden' fundamentals of 'how we do things round here' are questioned on a regular basis. Such questioning seems to be an essential component of 'double loop learning' or the re-framing essential to organizational transformation. You could institute your own management challenge and put in place this vital aspect of organizational learning by inviting different people in to question your operations. Why not start by inviting fellow managers from a sister plant? If you feel up to being more challenged than this you could invite a customer, a supplier or a stakeholder from the local community.

Source: Pedler Burgoyne and Boydell (1991)

How developers can help

If you find the above vision interesting, even compelling, you'll be wondering what you can do to contribute towards it. We think there are all kinds of possibilities and starting points. Some of the methods and ideas mentioned in earlier chapters are applicable here—such as self-development groups, or redeeming the practices of appraisal and goal setting by making them self-determined and by empowering the employee being appraised or setting the goals. The important thing is to do them while also being mindful of the whole company and, indeed, wider than that. 'Act locally; think globally' goes the ecological slogan, and it is something of this quality that characterizes people and their actions in the Learning Company.

Action learning is one of the methods that we think most appropriate to this perspective. We have discussed action learning as an approach in

Chapter 4. Although many people think of it as a training or development method involving groups of six or so managers with a 'set adviser', it is worth remembering that the founder of action learning, Reg Revans, has never restricted it in this way. He sees action learning as much more than mere method, more as a practical philosophy and a way of being and working together in the organization.

Revans' own description of the Learning Company was penned as long ago as 1969 when he described the characteristics of 'the enterprise as a learning system':

We observe that all expert systems here referred to must now be imposed upon the enterprise from above or from outside. But action learning must seek the means of improvement from within, indeed from the common task . . . the daily round offers constant learning opportunities . . . the quality of such learning is largely determined by the morale of the organisation . . .

(i) . . . that its chief executive places high among his own responsibilities that for developing the enterprise as a learning system: this he will achieve through his personal relations with his immediate subordinates . . .

(ii) . . . maximum authority for subordinates to act within the field of its own known policies that become known by interrogation from below . . .

(iii) . . . codes of practice . . . and other such regulations are to be seen as norms around which variations are deliberately encouraged as learning opportunities . . .

(iv) . . . any reference to what appears an intractable problem to a superior level should be accompanied both by an explanation why it cannot be treated where it seems to have arisen and a proposal to change the system so that similar problems arising in future could be suitably contained and treated . . .

(iv) . . . persons at all levels should be encouraged, with their immediate colleagues, to make regular proposals for the study and reorganisation of their own systems of work . . .

(Revans 1982, pp. 280–6)

If you want to follow the action learning path there are a number of sources of further information. Two of these are Revans 1983 and Pedler 1991.

Glimpses of the Learning Company

Here are two case studies in which some Learning Company principles are apparent.

Case study 1 Keatings of Mold, North Wales, is a small but rapidly expanding company that engraves cylinders for the printing of packagings of household name clients like Mars, Cadbury and Procter & Gamble. Before setting up his own company, Mike Keating had been managing director of a larger gravure company. He had learned from some of the mistakes of the past and was determined to improve on them. One view of his—echoed by many of the staff, who are paid the same high basic pay plus performance-related bonus—is that everyone should be doing the managing and there should be no designated managers apart from Mike and his fellow director, Phil.

Management development advisers introduced themselves and talked to all the 35 staff. From these discussions they identified a list of ways in which the running of the company could be improved. These ranged from improving the labelling of cylinders to computerizing the ever-shifting operating schedule; from more people needing to deal with customers to designing the layout of the new building.

The advisers suggested that everyone should be a member of a project team with others from different parts of the factory, as there were significant differences in terms of jobs, knowledge of the business and so on. Each person in the seven four-or-five person teams chose an individual task. Sometimes the whole team took on a joint task. Each group began with a two-hour session on how to work in a team and were helped to choose a coordinator, agree meeting times, target dates for completion, and so on. The task forces then met as and when they wished.

After three months most of the tasks had been completed. The results were impressive—not only in terms of improved supplier quality, better customer contact, computerization of the 'cutting list' and the other tasks, but also in terms of employees' abilities and willingness to take responsibility for managing. Many now felt they could take on jobs and responsibilities outside their job definitions and make a contribution to the whole company, although one or two felt their ideas were not really listened to by Mike and Phil.

At the same time there were many other initiatives going on in the company. Some of these came from the directors and some from the advisers. The directors took everyone, in two shifts, to the major European trade fair in Germany. The advisers started a multi-skilling programme.

To carry out the multi-skilling initiative, a list of all the jobs in the plant was drawn up: film making, engraving, proofing, plating, as well as accounting, sales and customer relations. All employees were asked to rate themselves against these jobs in four catagories—learner, competent worker, craftsperson and coach. Those who were really expert at the job in question were invited to become coaches and given tuition in coaching skills. Those who want to learn a given job are encouraged to find a coach and set up agreed times for learning. These can be short full-time attachments, but are more usually small amounts of time each day or on a regular weekly basis.

Another key activity is the education and feedback that the advisers provide to the top team. From the outset it has always been clear that Mike and Phil are the clients—it is their company. The advisers talk to them every day they are in the plant. Sometimes this is to pass on or gather news, sometimes to clear some course of action; but at other times it is to give feedback or introduce ideas. It comes as a shock to the directors, Mike and Phil—who put in long hours and look after their people well, paying them above average and so on—that some employees feel they are not listened to, or that something the directors are doing is unhelpful. Sometimes Mike and Phil would listen to this painful feedback—emerging perhaps from the results of a questionnaire or a series of shop floor meetings—and indicate that they didn't like it. The advisers would feel it wise to drop the subject but, often, a week or two later, they would hear that something had changed and that things had improved in this respect.

Every three or four months, the advisers held business planning seminars with the two directors. Off-site, in a pub, these would begin after a day's work and go on over beers and a meal until they were too tired to continue. They would re-start over bacon sandwiches at 8 a.m. the next day and end with a late lunch. As well as the normal business planning activities, these enjoyable and fairly free-form meetings would include short inputs on ideas from the advisers (e.g. on reward systems or the idea of partnerships) as well as occasions when the directors were given time for reflection on various issues and asked to present their findings to each other and have them critiqued. The period of about 18 months, over which this project has been operating, has seen big changes at Keatings—not least in the behaviour and policies of the directors. For example, Phil has joined a university management programme; Mike spends far more of his time with customers and off the plant than he would have thought possible.

Two comments on the Keatings case: first, not everything went as well as this short account may suggest. Some project teams didn't really deliver, the directors still don't listen equally to everyone, and so on. What is unmistakeable is the level of development—of individuals and of the company as a whole. The philosophy of 'everyone as a manager' and the efforts of the directors to provide development opportunities for all who want them will not only see some of the current operators in much bigger jobs but will allow Keatings to fulfil their ambitious plans for the future.

The second point is harder to answer: is this a Learning Company approach or just an example of a good training intervention, or perhaps a traditional organization development project? Learning Company ideas were used to create the vision of the future Keatings, and great efforts were put into trying to get everyone to participate in development and to put forward their ideas on future direction. Computerizing the cutting list was not only an example of 'informating' but also of power sharing. This was an important step, as the cutting list is the key control mechanism in Keatings and it was not easy for the directors to loosen their hold on it. At the same time, this handing over of control really makes managers of the operators and releases the directors for more customer contact and strategic thinking.

Having said all this, the question remains. A hallmark of a Learning Company approach is that it has aspirations not just for single loop learning—the continuous improvement of current operation—but also for double loop learning—the questioning of current operating norms and assumptions. This questioning leads to changes in these norms and is the key to the transformation of the whole. Also, that the approach encourages the company to develop the ability—as a whole organism—to learn how to learn, what Bateson (1986) called 'deutero-learning'. Evidence of this ability would mean that Keatings 'knew' how to do, not only single loop 'error correction and detection', but also double loop questioning and transformation of the current operating style and direction. This cannot be proved from the above case to date. There is plenty of evidence of single loop learning and some of double loop learning, but has the learning to learn capacity been developed?

Case study 2   Keatings is a small company where it is relatively easy to act locally while being mindful of the whole. This case study describes a project for improving patient care in a hospital, which is a much bigger and complex company.

Rivington General is a large hospital in a Yorkshire town of 250 000 people. Some 2½ years ago the Unit General Manager (UGM) and his management team introduced IPC—Individualized Patient Care—to the hospital and set up a development programme to improve the quality of care to the patient.

There are three elements in the programme—an IPC working party, which includes the UGM and senior nursing managers; an audit of 'ward atmosphere', and a course which is attended by the ward nursing managers (see Figure 5.3).

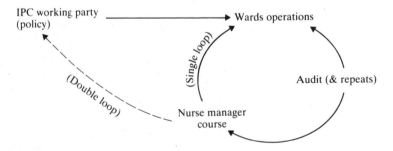

Figure 5.3   *Improving patient care*

Each ward is audited by research nurses using various scales to measure such things as:

• patient involvement in their own treatment
• the level of spontaneity and autonomy of patients
• the level of staff control

- the level of expressed anger and aggression
- the clarity of treatment programme goals and expectations
- the extent to which the patients' environment encourages them to prepare for life outside the hospital rather than becoming dependent.

Before attending the course, nurse managers have their wards audited and receive a report that shows the scores and also separates the views of patients, nurses, trainee nurses and doctors on all the items. There are often marked differences of view among these 'stakeholders'. The course consists of 12 × 2-hour sessions over a 4-month period and is designed to provide a forum for experienced nurses to examine their existing practice and to critique it. They are also asked to examine IPC ideas and practice and to feed this back to the working party.

As a result of the sessions, which include short inputs and some homework, but which operate more like quality circles or action learning groups, the nurse managers go back and implement whatever changes they think appropriate based on their analysis and discussion around the audit data. A further audit is carried out after 6 weeks and again after 6 months; it then becomes a regular yearly process.

After 2½ years and with the programme running continuously, some 8 courses have been held, and most wards show improvements on the various scales.

As Figure 5.3 shows, the IPC project at the hospital has created the opportunity for both single loop learning and double loop learning—if, in fact, the feedback from the nurse managers is strong enough to challenge and change current operating assumptions. In the Keatings case, this feedback was strengthened by having external advisers carry the messages. In the hospital, will the nurses say what they think to the IPC working party, which includes their senior managers, and, even if they do, will these senior people hear them?

Again we have plenty of evidence of single loop learning (which leads to better patient care and is, of course, very welcome), but less evidence of the double loop learning that carries the transformation opportunity. At this point, managers may say, with some justice: Why are you making such a fuss about this double loop and learning to learn capacity when we've improved matters for the customers—isn't that what matters? This is unarguable but the difference can perhaps be conveyed by the old saw—give someone food and you feed them for the day; teach them to fish and you feed them for ever. Not just learning *now* but acquiring the enhanced capacity to learn more in the *future* is the name of this game.

Following on from this perspective, the next section is concerned with a view of the company as a pattern of energy flows, where human and material energy is brought to bear on the issues of policy, learning, action and collective operations. In this view of organization, developers may find a role first of all in diagnosing and mapping the current pattern of energy flow and, second, in working with members of the company to balance, harmonize and redirect energy to the parts of the organization that are presently being starved or under-resourced.

The Learning Company as energy flow

The Learning Company is a new way of seeing organization not as a system of lines and boxes, or a complex of parts with feedback loops, as in the machine and systems metaphors, but as a flow of consciousness or energy. In this view of the organization (Pedler, Burgoyne and Boydell 1991) there are four double loops or figure eights, each of which represents vital aspects of functioning around which energy flows. These double loops are based on the idea of the unity of inner and outer—company and environment, person and problem, inner world and outer world. This is a 'both . . . and' view of the world rather than an 'either . . . or' view; one which is concerned with thinking about both at the same time, rather than focusing on this to the exclusion of that (see Figure 5.4).

Figure 5.4   *Balanced energy flow*

We have cited before Revans' remark that 'there is no learning without action, and no (sober and deliberate) action without learning' (1983, p. 54). Much of Revans's life has been given over to trying to convince us of the symbiotic nature of learning and action. He has railed against the splitting up of managing, where 'thinking' is seen as the preserve of the business schools and 'doing' the prerogative of managers in organizations. His action learning is designed to heal this split and restore our vision of 'both . . . and' thinking. Another of his formulations also shows this: 'Those unable to change themselves cannot change what goes on around them' (1983, p. 55); personal change and organizational change are not separate issues, they belong together, they require each other.

The double loop of inner and outer is central to this way of thinking. The loop cannot exist without both parts; you cannot have a one-sided coin. The loop connecting them is a path of energy flow, which is created and maintained by passing from one to the other and back again, making the two a unity, a synergy. The energy is created from the difference between the two, yet the two are not polarized but brought together in synergy. As long as the energy continues to flow from one to the other, we can be aware of the difference without allowing it to pull us apart. We can see another company as both competitor *and* colleague, as long as energy flows through one to the other and back again. If we fall into seeing this person as *either* this *or* that, then we lose this vision, this synergy.

So what are the four double energy loops of the Learning Company? The first two of these are 'horizontal' and represent the energy flow of the individual person from ideas to action and vice versa and the collective energy of the company between policy and operations and vice versa. The individual double loop we call the learning flow; the collective one is the strategic flow (see Figure 5.5).

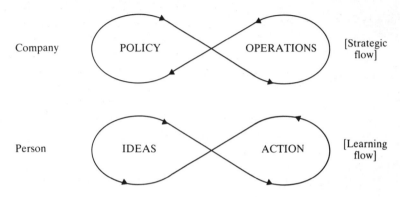

Figure 5.5   *Horizontal double energy loops*

The POLICY and IDEAS loops are inner in nature, while the OPERATIONS and ACTION loops are outer. To work in the way we have been describing, the Learning Company needs to have energy flowing from policy to operations and vice versa in an unbroken flow. Discussion of policy is energized by differences observed in operations, and operations are continually critiqued in the light of existing and emerging policy. Meanwhile, each person is engaged in learning and acting in the symbiotic sense described above by Revans. These two loops are strongly related to some of the characteristics outlined earlier, especially *learning approach to strategy* and *learning climate*.

However, for the Learning Company to come to life there must also be energy flows and connections between the individual and collective levels. This gives a second pair of 'vertical' double loops (see Figure 5.6).

The OPERATIONS and ACTION double loop is the one familiar to all managers and concerns the meshing of individual action with collective operations. This is the heart of the management of production—so much so that when we have talked about managing, we have tended to mean this coordination of individual actions into a whole operation. However, for the energy flow to work here, just as much effort must go into empowering people in their individual spheres of action as into the collective coordination and collaboration. People's needs to be effective actors (on the basis of their learning) must not be subordinated in any general sense to the need for collective coordination (based on collective policy).

The fourth and last double loop, POLICY and IDEAS, or participating flow is obviously related to the characteristic of participative policy making.

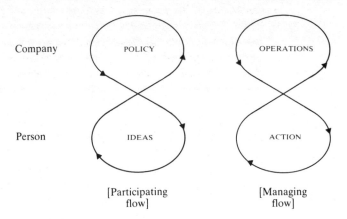

Company

Person

[Participating flow]   [Managing flow]

Figure 5.6   *Vertical double energy loops*

This is one of the keys to the Learning Company, being the most under-developed of all the double loops in many companies. Here the energy of people's ideas is harnessed at the collective policy-making level, and our corporate attempts at direction finding enrich and enable the quality of thinking and ideas for each person.

The four flows, or concerns, produced are an index to the development of thinking about managing. In line with our earlier description of the evolution of the Learning Company, we can portray these as successive challenges which those concerned with managing were called upon to meet. Thus:

1 The first is the *managing* flow, concerning the efficient and effective operation of the production unit. Towards the end of the nineteenth century and in the early years of the twentieth, this was the first challenge to be overcome with the help of thinkers like Henri Fayol. This challenge gave us the definition of managing as being about planning, controlling, motivating, coordinating and so on. (An interesting possibility is that the Workers Control movement, which was very active at the same time, forms an antithesis to this managerialist 'revolution'.)

2 The second flow, or challenge, is *strategic* where, having gained control of internal production, managing becomes preoccupied with direction finding and the struggle to control or, at least, to respond to the 'turbulence' or unpredictability of the environment in which the company operates. The POLICY loop is thus concerned with looking outwards and upwards, trying to see into an uncertain future, watching competitors and markets closely, in order to decide how best to secure survival and growth. This challenge has preoccupied managers in the second half of the twentieth century after the loss of stable, colonial markets and aided by thinkers such as Burns and Stalker (1959), with their typology of mechanistic and organismic organizations, Chandler (1962), with this seminal work on strategy and structure, and, more recently, Mintzberg (1979) and Porter (1982).

3 The third challenge is to do with *learning* and grows directly out of the second. As we have noted above, acquiring the capacity to learn at individual and collective levels is the best way of ensuring a developing strategy that is appropriate to the times. This challenge is the one we are facing now and to which the Learning Company is one response. After understanding how to manage production and getting a grip on strategy, managers are now faced with the task of facilitating this learning capacity in people and organizations. The thinkers who have pointed to this have been mentioned and include Argyris, Schon, Deming and Revans.

4 The fourth challenge is that of *participation* and, together with the other three, completes the transformation of our view of organization from the pyramid controlled from the top to the energetic collaboration of 'companions' envisaged by the Learning Company. In our experience this is the challenge that frightens managers most— the memory of the Workers Control movement resurfaces, perhaps? People who are prepared to contemplate the creation of learning opportunities for all company members, and to strive towards their vision of a Learning Company, draw back from the notion of widespread participation in decision making and/or ownership. It is indeed a demanding task. Nevertheless, our vision of the Learning Company requires this nettle to be grasped—in order to harness all the learning being done in the company; in order to make the best decisions about the future of the company as a whole; in order for everyone to do their best work and make the best contribution to the whole, methods and systems that enable everyone to participate in these matters must be devised.

The movement for Total Quality Management requires a high level of participation, consultation and collaboration. This approach to managing production is a transformation of the old managerial preoccupation with control, which requires people to be self-directing and self-controlling in order to do their best work.

There are various authors who have pioneered the *participation* flow, especially within the co-operative movement; they include amongst other industrialists such as Wilfred Brown, Ernest Bader (Davis, 1991); also Revans and Deming where widespread participation is implicit in their ideas.

Activity 5.2 *Mapping energy flow in your company*

Putting these four challenges and four double loops together gives us an energy flow model with a number of interesting possibilities. Imagine the four double loops all connecting with, and flowing through, each other so that, for example, the strategic flow between Policy and Operations, and vice versa, mingles at the Policy end with the participation flow between Ideas and Policy and vice versa; and also with the managing flow between Action and Operations and vice versa. Obviously, the learning flow is similarly connected with the participation and managing flows, so that we can think of the company as an organism that aims to direct and draw energy to and from these four flows in a balanced, harmonious and ceaseless fashion (see Figure 5.7).

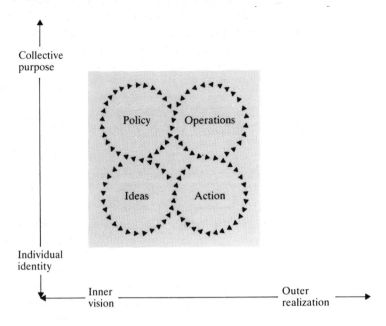

Figure 5.7 The company as energy flow

1 Consider your own organization in this light. Where does your company put its collective energy? What flows are neglected? What loops are emphasized to the exclusion of their partnering loop?
2 When you've thought about this, in the space below draw the diagram shown in Figure 5.7 to simulate energy flow in your own company. Draw thick, thin, and dotted lines (or leave the lines out) to show where energy is expended and drawn from.

It may help in doing this if you can visualize your company and its energy flows. Imagine all the members of the company walking round the various loops and flows in the diagram. Do they form a well-balanced, harmonious and seamless flow? Or do they congregate around particular areas with little or no energy in others?

3 One way in which you can take your diagnosis further and begin to try to change things is to get a number of volunteers from the company and, on a suitable occasion, actually walk around the shape shown in Figure 5.7. You may need to do this in several stages. Divide the company into four and get them first to practise walking round one double loop each. Have them try to balance and harmonize the flow between two loops, becoming aware when they move from one preoccupation into another.

When they can walk their double loop without too much difficulty, get them to mesh with one other double loop, so that the original four groups are now working in two halves, sharing one loop in common and retaining the other alone. The third stage is to mesh these two together so that the whole company is following the model above, each loop being shared by two of the original four groups, each of which is treading its particular flow.

If the members can regulate the four meshing flows reasonably well, a further challenge is to ask them to make variations—either individual ones where people move out of their original flow and into another, or collective, where the company concentrates more resources in one area than in another. You can get people to practise this shifting and collective control of energy for as long as they will put up with it. Because we are concerned about energy—its generation, expenditure and balanced flow—it is important to find a way of working that simulates this. Walking or dancing is one way of doing it, but there will be others.

4 Ask people to share their experience of this and also of the company in the light of the idea. In their working lives, do people feel confined to one loop or another, or is there free movement for all? Do we divide ourselves up between 'thinkers' and 'doers', 'managers' and 'managed', 'learners' and 'plodders', or in any of the other great variety of ways we have for dividing ourselves?

Can we get energy concentrated in particular flows when we need to, or is the company rather rigid and inflexible in the way it operates? Are our relationships such that, like a black hole, they absorb light and energy, or are they energizing in themselves, a source of enjoyment and innovation?

We hope you manage to get something going in your company, with or without the aid of this model and the 'formation dancing'. We end here some way from where we started but in the belief that developers who are concerned to help themselves and others to develop should devote some of their attention to the company as a whole and not just restrict themselves to individuals and groups. It is the Learning Company that creates the best conditions for self-development. In fact, the Learning Company is the ideal home for self-developers—a company fit to house the spirit of the developing person. As developers we all work where we can, where the client is, where the energy is, but the Learning Company beckons as a worthy, if lofty, ambition.

References

Argyris, C. and D. A. Schon (1978) *Organisational Learning: A Theory in Action Perspective*, Addison-Wesley, Mass, USA.

Bateson, G. (1986) *Steps to an Ecology of Mind*, Paladin, London.

Brown, W. (1971) *Organisation*, Heinemann, London.

Burns, T. and N. Stalker (1959) *The Management of Innovation*, Tavistock, London.

Chandler, A. (1962) *Strategy and Structure*, Doubleday, NY.

Davis, J. (1991) *Greening Business: Managing for sustainable development*, Blackwell, Oxford, pp. 142–3.

Deming, W. E. (1988) *Out of the Crisis*, Cambridge University Press, Cambridge.

Gergen, K. (1978) 'Towards Generative Theory', *Journal of Personality and Social Psychology*, 36, pp. 1344–60.

Hamel, G and C. K. Prahalad (1989) 'Strategic Intent', *Harvard Business Review*, May-June, pp. 63–76.

McCaskey, M. (1988) 'The Challenge of Managing Ambiguity and Change', in Pondy, Boland and Thomas (eds), *Managing Ambiguity and Change*, pp. 1–15, Wiley, Chichester, UK.

McConnell, D. and V. Hodgson (1990) 'Computer Mediated Communications Systems (CMCS)—Electronic Networking and Education', *Management Education and Development*, 21(1), Spring, pp. 51–8.

Mintzberg, H. (1979) *The Structure of Organizations*, Prentice-Hall, Englewood Cliffs, NJ.

Pedler, M. J. (1991) *Action Learning in Practice* (2nd ed.) Gower Press, Aldershot, UK.

Pedler, M. J. and T. H. Boydell (1990) *Managing Yourself*, Gower Press, Aldershot, UK.

Pedler, M. J., T. H. Boydell and J. G. Burgoyne (1988) 'Learning Company Project Report', *Training Agency* Sheffield, UK, May.

Pedler, M. J., T. H. Boydell and J. G. Burgoyne (1989) 'Towards the Learning Company', *Management Education and Development*, 20(1), pp. 1–8.

Pedler, M.J., J. G. Burgoyne and T. H. Boydell (1991) *The Learning Company: A Strategy for Sustainable Development*, McGraw-Hill, Maidenhead, UK.

Peters, T. J. and R. H. Waterman, Jr. (1982) *In Search of Excellence: Lessons from America's Best-Run Companies*, Harper and Row, NY.

Porter, M. (1982) *Competitive Strategy*, Macmillan, NY.

Revans, R. W. (1982) *The Origins and Growth of Action Learning*, Chartwell-Bratt, Bromley, UK.

Revans, R. W. (1983) *The ABC of Action Learning*, Chartwell-Bratt, Bromley, UK.

6 Resources for self-development

Where do I go from here?—the self-developer's perennial question. Chapter 6 provides one description of the range of education, training and development activities that are relevant to developers working with individuals, groups and organizations.

Our field is characterized by a rich diversity of approaches, methods, philosophies, techniques and ideas about human and organizational development. This very richness has its down side. Many of us fall into bee-like behaviour, sipping momentarily from every available flower and never settling for long anywhere. A balance needs to be sought between the urge to explore what is a truly wondrous variety and the need to work deeply from a well-considered position.

Developmental route map

For the new developer there is simply the problem of where to start. To this problem we have no easy answer. What we have chosen to do is to present some sixty approaches that we have arranged into 12 streams. We stress from the outset that this is only a snapshot of the developer's universe and not one that we would wish to label authoritative. Like early maps of the New World it is designed to give you a start and encourage you to go further. If, on your travels to date, you have encountered streams or approaches that we have not included, we would like to hear from you. In this way, future maps may be more complete.

An overview of the approaches is given in Figure 6.1. This list is an early version of a survey conducted by Transform: Individual and Organisation Development Ltd. as part of the 'Developing the Developers' project on behalf of the Association of Management Education and Development (AMED) and the Employment Department. The bibliography presented in this chapter is part of a wider bibliography compiled as part of this project. We are grateful to AMED for permission to use this material.

The overview in Figure 6.1 is sorted into 12 columns, or streams, and four rows, which we call 'eras'. The streams show a group of approaches that we see as being clearly linked and developing out of

STREAMS

ERA	A Text-based learning	B Systematic	C Therapy	D On-job development	E Whole-person development	F Spiritual development	G Physical development	H Equal opportunities
Pre-1965 **Pre-Scientific**	A1 Correspondence courses	B1 Job analysis	C1 Tavistock	D1 Apprenticeship	E1 Adult education	F1 Moral management	G1 Muscular Christianity	H1 Cultural assimilation
1965–75 **Systematic**	A2 Programmed learning	B2 Systematic training	C2 Humanistic psychology, Body-work, Gestalt	D2 Instruction	E2 Action learning	F2 Meditation	G2 Outward Bound	H2 Racism/sexism awareness training
1975–85 **Business-oriented**	A3 Open/distance learning	B3 Training by objectives	C3 Radical therapy, Co-counselling, TA, Assertion, Time management	D3 Coaching	E3 Self-development	F3 Corporate responsibility	G3 Outdoor development, Artistic expression	H3 Women's/men's development and multiculturalism
1985 – > **Holistic**	A4 Integrated programmes	B4 Competencies	C4 NLP, Stress management	D4 Mentoring	E4 Education for all	F4 Values/ethics, Green organization, Spirituality	G4 Total well-being	H4 Flexible firm/HRD strategy

Figure 6.1 *Approaches to development*

	Focal group	Group training	Organizational	Strategy development	Quality	Ownership	Technology
	I	J	K	L	M	N	O

I1 Supervisors	J1 T-groups	K1 Survey feedback	L1 Policy making	M1 Inspection	N1 Welfarism	O1 Mechanization
I2 Graduates	J2 Encounter, Structured experiences	K2 Organization development	L2 MBO	M2 Quality control	N2 Co-ops/autonomous work groups	O2 Group technology
I3 Middle managers	J3 Team building	K3 Excellence	L3 Business planning	M3 Quality assurance	N3 Wider share ownership	O3 Automation
I4 Everyone a manager	J4 Networking/cross-functional groups	K4 Organization transformation, Learning Company	L4 Strategy formation	M4 TQM	N4 Stakeholder relations	O4 Integrated manufacture

	Converging professions	Developing developers
	P	Q

P1 Teaching, Personnel, Administration	Q1 Ad-hoc
P2 Training, social work	Q2 Introductory training officer courses
P3 Line management	Q3 Foundation programmes for trainers (Harper Report)
P4 Strategy quality	Q4 Management learning/developing developers

each other in sequence over time. So, for example, open and distance learning is a descendant of programmed learning and, earlier still, of correspondence courses.

Two streams—P and Q—are detached from the others because we see them as somewhat different. The gap between these two and the other approaches symbolizes the incompleteness of our list.

The eras are a way of seeing the development of ideas over time. They express when the approaches first had an impact on the field of development, so you can expect that your own chronology may differ from that in the figure. Some of the approaches from earlier eras are still alive and well, and of use to us and, we are sure, to many of you.

Most of what is written about training and development approaches emerged after the UK Industrial Training Act of 1964, which introduced the Industrial Training Boards and ushered in the era of systematic training. However, most of these approaches grew out of streams that had their sources further back into the hills of time, before the widespread growth of the training and development 'profession'. The two more recent eras contain approaches which have emerged from the earlier forms over the last twenty years.

Clearly, our chronology is questionable, and it is perhaps not surprising that these eras coincide with our own development, as we both entered the world of work in the mid-1960s. So, it is clear to us that approaches to development can only be catalogued and boxed for a specific and limited purpose.

Our purpose is to provide a guide to resources and a 'developmental route map' which you can use to plan the next phase of your journey. Developers, as people, typically range widely, borrow eclectically, pick up tools and ideas, and make their own meaning as they go along. This chapter offers three things:

1 a map of the field
2 a description of each approach
3 indicative references for each approach

The descriptions and references follow, and these may give you a start, a toe-hold, in any approach you would like to discover more about. Before moving on to these, here is a route map activity.

Activity 6.1 *My own developmental route map*

1 Using Figure 6.1 (you may wish to make a copy of it), trace the development of your own ideas to date. Put a red asterisk (*) in up to twelve boxes that you have 'visited' and which have contributed to your way of working. We suggest a limit of 12 asterisks to help focus on those approaches that have clearly influenced your current practice as a developer.
2 Can you link your asterisks in sequence, showing your point of origin and the route and any branches you have taken since?

3 What does the route tell you about your experience and preferred ways of working? At this point you could ask one or more of your colleagues to try the activity and compare your route with theirs. Do the different routes illuminate contrasts in how you approach development?

4 Now look at the map again. This time put a green asterisk in each of the boxes you would like to visit next. *Limit yourself to six at most.*

5 Make a start on your further self-development by picking one of the green asterisks and going straight to the appropriate descriptions that make up the rest of this chapter. You will find a reference or two to help you explore the area further. There will be other references in the stream that you may find useful if you wish to look more widely. As well as books we have included recent articles, audio tapes and videotapes.

Approaches and references

Development is a complex and living process, and a history of development will not necessarily do justice to all this rich complexity. Nonetheless the models presented below are more elaborate than many of the elegant models in the literature (Lessem 1989; Pedler, Burgoyne and Boydell 1991).

We have gone for a relatively high degree of complexity because we needed our model to contain descriptions of development that would be recognizable to developers as terms they would use to describe their own work.

The basic model has three kinds of component:

- **streams**, which collect together a strand in the development of developers;
- **eras**, the four periods through which each of the streams evolved during the last 50 years; and
- **approaches**, which describe how each stream was manifested in a particular era.

These components, brought together, create the matrix which is our basic model of development, and is shown in Figure 6.1.

Streams in development

The streams listed are broad ways of thinking about and carrying out development. Some of them are predominantly *individual*, in that the recipients of the development are individuals even though they may be receiving the development in the presence of others. In other cases, the stream is primarily *group* based, in that learning takes place through group interaction, and the outcome of the learning is primarily about the group, rather than the individual. Yet other approaches are *organizational*, in that the focus is on larger chunks of the organization than face-to-face groups, or it addresses some aspect of the organization as a whole. Many of the organization approaches are interesting in that the primary impulse for their adoption in organizations comes not from developers, but from others in the organization, e.g. technologists or strategists. The column headed 'Era' in Figure 6.1 describes the controlling idea or paradigm that was emerging at that time; Column P, headed 'Converging professions', lists some of the occupations that developers came from; and Column Q, headed 'Developing developers', describes the dominant approach to development of developers at that time.

The streams are categorized as follows:

Individual streams

A   Text-based learning
B   Systematic
C   Therapy
D   On-job development
E   Whole-person development
F   Spiritual development
G   Physical approaches
H   Equal opportunities
I   Focal group

Group streams

J   Group training

Organization streams

K   Organizational
L   Strategy development
M   Quality
N   Ownership
O   Technology

First, each stream is described, and then each of the approaches within the stream is specified. If there is more than one approach in any era, each approach is described separately. Then, for each approach, you are offered one or more resources to pursue any interest that you might have in that area. Each resource has a brief annotation indicating its use to developers. The reference and annotation will make it clear whether the resource is

- a book
- a chapter from a book
- an article
- an audio tape
- a videotape

A mixture of all these types of resource is included.

Individual streams

A Text-based learning   Developing and/or using texts, often programmed and requiring learning activity, including individual counselling of participants in a learning centre, where they are working independently at their own pace. Text includes learning material presented through computer-based media.

Mann, S. J. *et al.* (1987) *The Effective Design and Delivery of Open and Distance Learning for Management Education,* Centre for the Study of Management Learning, University of Lancaster, and Manpower Services Commission, Sheffield. March.

A study of what happened to two open and distance learning packages for management education in two large organizations. In one, out of 230 people who received the package, only 13 completed it. Contains excellent guidelines on how to introduce and support open and distance learning in order to get results. Open and distance learning emerges as *not* a cheap option.

A1 Correspondence courses
Developing and/or tutoring programmes where contact between tutor and learners is by correspondence—in the past, usually mail, but currently also by electronic mail.

A2 Programmed learning
Developing and/or tutoring programmes that have been developed with tightly defined learning objectives, and are tested by participant response to questions posed in the text. Participants work independently at their own pace, but may come to the developer for tutorial assistance.

Page, T. and Q. A. Whitlock (eds) (1979) *Aspects of Educational Technology: Volume XIII,* Kogan Page, London. Conference papers from the very end of the programmed learning era.

A3.1 Open learning
Designing and/or delivering a learning system that is structured to minimize barriers to entry, such as access to teacher, time of study period, entry qualification.

Lewis, R. (1986) 'What is open learning?' *Open Learning,* June, pp. 5–10. A helpful summary of the difference between closed and open learning, exploring barriers and limits to openness.

Mann, S. (1988) 'Why open learning can be a turn-off', *Personnel Management,* 20(1), January, pp. 41–3. A more candid and less optimistic review of the topic.

Fuller, A. and M. Saunders (1990) 'The paradox of open learning at work', *Personnel Review,* 19(5), pp. 29–33. Explores three paradoxical imperatives of open learning—access, empowerment and cost effectiveness, using a case study of a retail company.

A3.2 Distance learning
A new name for A1, often involving computer-mediated communication.

Hodgson, V. *et al.* (eds) (1987) *Beyond Distance Teaching—Towards Open Learning,* Society for Research into Higher Education and Open University Press, Milton Keynes, UK. A collection of papers concerned with issues in open and distance learning. Covers use of new technology as well as defining the terms, the problems and some of the solutions.

A4.1   Computer-based training
Designing and/or delivering training that uses computers to present and log learning, determine the path through the material, and trigger use of other media (as in interactive video, where the computer activates a laser-read disk to present a scene on video).

Harrison, N. (1990) *How to design Effective Computer-Based Training: A Modular Course*, McGraw-Hill, Maidenhead. A systematic guide to the process of designing CBT. The self-development comes in the use of the medium.

Krut, R. and M. Bulgen (1990) 'Changing managers' behaviour through computer simulations', *Personnel Management*, 22(5), May, pp. 61–3. Illustrations of a wide range of areas of management development in Chase Manhatten Bank.

A4.2   Integrated programmes
Open learning packages that adopt a whole-person approach (see Stream E) and integrate learning and work (see Approach E2).

Binsted, D. (1986) *Developments in Interpersonal Skills Training*, Gower, Aldershot, UK. A monograph that lays out clearly the fruits of Don Binsted's work on interactive skills training, often using interactive video. Contains clear models and strategies for skills development together with self-development activities.

First Line Manager (1990), Intek, London. A structured programme for first line manager development including text, self-development tasks, organizational projects and learning sets.

B   Systematic
One strand of development is the impulse to order the world, and to specify in great detail what must be learned, either for an individual job-holder or for a whole category of people (e.g. all managers).

B1   Job analysis
The armed forces were among the leaders in analysing and specifying what had to be learned in order to carry out tasks and whole jobs.

Campbell, C. P. (1989) 'Job analysis for industrial training', *Journal of European Industrial Training*, 13(2). Whole edition dedicated to developments in technique and application.

B2   Systematic training
The Training Boards adopted this approach and broadened it to embrace organizational needs as well as job needs.

Fairbairns, J. (1991) 'Plugging the gap in training needs analysis', *Personnel Management*, 23(2), February, pp. 43–5. A brilliant analysis of the weakness of traditional training needs analysis; provides a mechanism for introducing the missing cultural dimension.

B3 Training by objectives
With a more businesslike orientation, this approach was transformed into a focus on meeting objectives, rather than carrying out tasks.

Novack, K. M. (1991) 'A true training needs analysis', *Training and Development Journal*, 45(4), April, pp. 69–74. Makes the differentiation between needs and wants in a straightforward, businesslike way.

Mager, R. F. and P. Pipe (1984) *Analyzing Performance Problems*, Pitman, Belmont, Ca. Focuses on performance problems rather than training needs.

B4 Competences
A return to the job focus, but emphasizing what can be done rather than what is known. A strong emphasis on common needs for all managers at a certain stage in their career.

Training and Development Lead Body (1991) *National Standards for Training and Development*, Employment Department, Sheffield. An example of the competencies approach applied to the role of training and development. Very clear descendant of the systematic training approach with hierarchical analysis starting from Key Purpose ('Develop Human Potential to assist organisations and individuals to achieve their objectives'), Key Roles, Units of Competence and Elements.

Burgoyne, J. (1989) 'Creating the Managerial Portfolio: Building on Competency Approaches to Management', *Management Education and Development*, 20(1), Spring, pp. 56–61. Excellent short paper defining competency and listing eight problems that competence-based schemes of development must overcome. Essential reading.

C   Therapy
Therapeutic approaches to individual development began in the 1950s to move from an exclusive concern with 'sick' people to deal also with 'normal neurotics'. It was recognized that the unconscious plays a part in influencing the behaviour of even the best-adapted to everyday life. Therapeutic approaches recognize the relevance of these deep-seated impulses and enable learners to bring them into awareness and to make conscious choices about how to respond to them.

C1   Tavistock
The Tavistock Institute of Human Relations developed methods of working, first, with groups of sick people, and then with groups that function normally, and then with organizations (the sociotechnical approach). They developed the British T-group (see J1), and all their methods are characterized by trainers taking a rather formal and distant role reminiscent of the traditional therapist.

Banet, A. G. and C. Hayden (1977) 'A Tavistock Primer' in *The 1977 Annual Handbook for Group Facilitators*, University Associates, La Jolla, Ca. USA, pp. 155–66. Excellent short introduction to the central ideas of the Tavistock approach, interpretative and rooted in psychoanalytic theory revealing 'the hidden, sometimes sinister, irrational processes that affect individuals in group life'.

Miller, E. J. (1989) *The Leicester Model: Experiential Study of Group and Organisational Processes*, Occasional Paper No. 10, Tavistock Institute of Human Relations, London. Useful but at times difficult-to-read monograph sketching the history and theory of the famous Tavistock 'large group' Conference. Worth working at.

C2.1   Humanistic psychology
Combining Carl Roger's client-centred therapy and the National Training Laboratories T-group technology led to a group approach to helping people get in touch with their feelings and express them in an allegedly safe forum.

Rogers, C. (1978) *Carl Rogers on Personal Power*, Constable, London. The most politically aware of all Rogers's writing.

C2.2   Bodywork
A number of approaches emerged recognizing that free expression was inhibited by physical blocks that had become locked into skeleton or musculature. These approaches offered a range of methods from gentle postural awareness techniques (e.g. bioenergetics) through to deep massage (e.g. Reichian therapy).

Stuart, R. and S. Cotter (1988) 'Releasing Managers' Personal Energy', *Management Education and Development*, 19(1), Spring, pp. 4–21. How to rediscover, gain access to, mobilize and release your personal energy, based on the theories of Reich and Lowen.

Lowen, A. (1976) *Bioenergetics*, Penguin, Harmondsworth, UK. The basic source book on bioenergetics.

Ernst, S. and L. Goodison (1981) *In our own Hands: a Book of Self-help Therapy*, Women's Press, London. Excellent manual of self-development and group activities designed for women's groups but useful to men too. Not limited to bodywork activities, but there are several of these.

C2.3   Gestalt
Gestalt combined body awareness with psychological processes in a powerful way, and was used in organization development as well as individual development.

Perls, F. S. (1971) *Gestalt Therapy Verbatim*, Bantam, NY. Compiled after Perls's death from transcripts of some of his last sessions. Conveys the power and anarchy of his approach more immediately than Perls, Hefferline and Goodman's classic text.

Herman, S. M. and M. Korenich (1977) *Authentic management: A Gestalt Orientation to Organizations and their Development*, Addison-Wesley, Reading, Mass. Applying Gestalt ideas in an organization context.

C3.1   Radical therapy
Radical therapists combined the insights of Freud with those of Marx

and other socialist thinkers, to provide an organizational critique as well as individual insights.

Southgate, J. and R. Randall (1978) *The Barefoot Psychoanalyst*, Publications' Distributive Cooperative, London. A helpful and creative manual using words and pictures to 'initiate psychoanalytic self-help groups among ordinary people'. A similar picture-book exists for *Cooperative and Community Dynamics*.

C3.2   Co-counselling and other counselling approaches
Co-counselling or re-evaluation counselling was developed as a mutual support process, where two people take turns to be counsellor and counsellee. Emphasizes the discharge of emotion, to free the counsellee from past distress.

Jackins, H. (1973) *The Human Situation*, Rational Island, Seattle. A co-counselling classic.

Heron, J. (1990) *Helping the Client: A Creative, Practical Guide*, Sage, London. John Heron's Six Category Intervention Analysis, which can be used in any form of counselling. A good framework for analysing behaviour and making interventions.

Heron, J. (1981) 'Self and Peer Assessment' in Boydell, T. and M. Pedler (eds) *Management Self-Development: Concepts and Practices*, Gower, Aldershot, pp. 111–28. How to do peer reviews, drawn from experience in working with doctors on medical audit but widely applicable to any professional self and peer review process.

C3.3   Transactional Analysis
In many ways a popularization of traditional therapeutic models, TA added insights about the game-like nature of much interaction, and provided an accessible language for managers to explore their own and others' behaviour.

Jongward, D. and M. James (1971) *Born to Win*, Addison-Wesley, Englewood Cliffs, NJ. Good introduction to the principles of transactional analysis with lots of activities and exercises.

C3.4   Assertiveness
Another interactive approach, emphasizing how our own behaviour can influence the response we receive. Widely used in single-gender work, as men and women were seen to face different issues around assertion.

Back, K. and J. Back (1982) *Assertiveness at Work*, McGraw-Hill, Maidenhead. Of the very many books and articles on assertiveness, this is one that has lasted well.

Dickson, A. (1982) *A Woman in Your Own Right*, Quartet. Strongly written primer which has that extra edge by being written for women.

C3.5   Time management
Included as a therapeutic approach because, at best, it goes beyond

merely 'being better organized' to looking at the deeper impulses that reduce our ability to use our time well.

Davidson, J. (1978) *Effective Time Management: A Practical Workbook*, Human Sciences Press, London. One of the better and shorter workbooks in the overpopulated time management field. Large format.

Garratt, S. (1985) *Manage Your Time*, Fontana, London. A manager's handbook, straightforward and sensible. Less of a workbook than Davidson, but lots of examples.

BBC Training Videos (1988) *The Time Manager*, BBC, London: 25 minute video; helpful in that it links work and home.

Kotter, J. (1982) *The General Managers*, McGraw-Hill, NY. Contains a salutary reminder that some of the more simplistic solutions offered in the above sources run counter to what successful executives actually do.

C4.1   Neurolinguistic programming (NLP)
A powerful integration of mind and body awareness, using an intriguing cinematographic metaphor of thinking (changing the pictures on the screen of your mind's eye) to yield rapid and potent changes.

Gastner, D. (1988) 'NLP—a practical technology for trainers', *Training Officer*, February. A straightforward reference to this topic.

Bandler, R. and J. Grinder (1982) *Reframing*, Real People Press, Utah. A practical text by the founders of this method, which claims to offer a set of skills and operating principles for effecting improved communication and personal change.

C4.2   Stress management
Recognizing that psychological pressure has physiological effects, and development requires multi-faceted lifestyle changes.

Cooper, C. L. and M. Davidson (1982) *High Pressure: Working Lives of Women Managers*, Fontana, London. Accessible paperback with lots of illustrations and exercises. Aimed at women managers but valuable to men too.

Pedler, M. and T. Boydell (1985) *Managing Yourself*, Fontana, London. A broad self-management approach to stress—a healthy life is one in which you manage your health through knowing and valuing yourself. Lots of illustrations and self-development activities.

D   On-job development
The recognition that one of the principal forums for development is work itself (you don't have to go on a course to learn things). Line managers can generate this kind of learning, and so can offline managers, who can be charged with this special responsibility.

Megginson, D. (1988) 'Instructor, coach, mentor: three ways of helping for managers', *Management Education & Development*, 19(1), Spring, pp.

33–46. A comparison of these three approaches linked to a model of individual development.

Mumford, A. (1980) *Making Experience Pay*, McGraw-Hill, Maidenhead. A book aimed at managers, about learning from the immediate work experience. Lots of ideas about how to make your work a learning-full environment.

Manpower Services Commission (1987) *Managing Learning: The Vital Role of the Line Manager*, Video Arts, London. A video and booklet outlining the case for manager involvement and citing some examples—British Steel, W. H. Smith, Yorkshire Water and British Aerospace.

D1   Apprenticeship
Learning at work seen as largely informal, based on serving time, and being around an acknowledged professional or qualified expert.

Liepman, K. (1960) *Apprenticeship: An Enquiry into its Adequacy under Modern Conditions*, Routledge and Kegan Paul, London. An interesting case of *déjà vu*.

Engineering Industry Training Board (1985) 'Recent developments in engineering education and training in the UK', *Journal of European Industrial Training*, 9(6), pp. 17–22. A good review of the then deplorable state of apprenticeship. It was hard to believe how much worse it was going to get.

D2   Instruction
Learning at work seen as requiring a systematic breakdown of the tasks and skills needed to perform the job. These can then be taught and practised in a deliberate and focused way.

Mager, R. F. (1988) *Making Instruction Work*, Pitman, London. An updated classic, with not much emphasis on development.

Wlodkowski, R. J. (1985) *Enhancing Adult Motivation to Learn*, Jossey-Bass, San Francisco, Ca. Sophisticated and enormously detailed analysis of the range of interventions that a trainer can make; with a developmental focus.

D3   Coaching
A process in which a manager, through direct discussion and guided activity, helps a colleague to solve a problem or do a task better (Megginson and Boydell 1979).

Megginson, D. and T. Boydell (1979) *A Manager's Guide to Coaching*, BACIE, London. A user's guide to the organizational contexts and individual skills required for coaching.

Phillips, K. R. (1987) *Coaching Skills Inventory*, MLR Ltd, Carmarthen. A situation-based self-diagnostic questionnaire, leading to a six-stage model of the coaching process.

Halson, B. (1990) 'Teaching supervisors to coach', *Personnel Management*,

22(3), March, pp. 36–9, 53. An approach to self-organized learning in the Post Office.

Video Arts (1990) *The Helping Hand*, Video Arts, London. The John Cleese treatment for coaching, using a five-step model.

D4 Mentoring
A process in which a mentor helps learners to build their life's work. The focus is on the learner's development and concerns, helping the learner through life crises or into new stages of development.

Clutterbuck, D. (1991) *Everyone needs a Mentor* (2nd ed.), IPM, London. An updated edition of this classic in the field.

Wright, R. G. and W. B. Werther Jnr (1991) 'Mentors at work', *Journal of Management Development*, 10(3), pp. 25–32. A useful survey of the American literature on mentoring.

Daloz, L. A. (1986) *Effective Teaching and Mentoring*, Jossey-Bass, San Francisco. A fascinating journey, involving myth, children's stories and Dante's *Inferno*, as well as recent research results.

E Whole-person development
This approach focuses on the person of the learner, rather than the pre-planned curriculum of the developer or the needs 'of the organization'. Developers using this approach are interested in enabling learners to identify their own needs, and often to plan the means of meeting them.

E1 Adult education
Many university extramural tutors and some, but by no means all, college or adult centre lecturers fall into this category. To do so they have to adopt a learner-centred approach.

Brookfield, S. (1987) *Creating Dynamic Adult Learning Experiences*, Jossey-Bass, San Francisco. Audio-cassette interviews of some of the luminaries of adult learning, including Knowles and Wlodkowski.

Knowles, M. S. (1970) *The Modern Practice of Adult Education*, Association Press, NY. An old but excellent book outlining Malcolm Knowles's pragmatic but theory-based approach to adult learning. Lots of case examples and how-to-do-its.

Schein, E. (1978) *Career Dynamics: Matching Individual and Organisational Needs*, Addison-Wesley, Reading, Mass. Looks at development needs in the adult (male?) career/life cycle and how these fit together with organizational requirements.

Lievegoed, B. (1979) *Phases: Crisis and Development in the Individual*, Steiner Press, London. A biographical approach to human development looking at needs in various life phases based on Rudolf Steiner's ideas. See Gail Sheehy's *Passages: Predictable Crises in Adult Life*, Bantam, New York, for a North American equivalent.

Department of Adult and Higher Education, University of Manchester, Manchester M13 9LP. Has a list of monographs and occasional papers on many practical and theoretical issues in adult education.

E2   Action learning

Helping managers to work in sets to challenge and support each other in carrying out a demanding project designed to stimulate both organizational improvement and personal learning.

Revans, R. W. (1983) *The ABC of Action Learning*, Chartwell-Bratt. Bromley. The primer from the master. Short, but everything is here if you look carefully.

Pedler, M. J. (1991) *Action Learning in Practice* (2nd ed.), Gower Press, Aldershot, UK. Wide-ranging collection of papers, including some classics, on all aspects of action learning with an emphasis on application in various settings.

Revans, R. *Action Learning*, video from IMCB. An interview with Reg Revans. Revans argues that in a changing world people should be masters in the art of questioning, i.e. have the skill to ask questions to solve problems, thus learning while working. The main points of this film come across well, after Revans's introduction and history has been sat through.

E3   Self-development

Those approaches to management training and development that seek to increase the ability and willingness of managers to take responsibility for themselves, particularly for their own learning (Pedler, Burgoyne and Boydell 1988).

Pedler, M. J., J. E. Burgoyne and T. H. Boydell (1986) *A Manager's Guide to Self-Development* (2nd ed.), McGraw-Hill, Maidenhead, UK. A 'doing' book with a clear underlying philosophy that contains analytical tools and activities for self-development. User-friendly.

Kemp, N. J. (1989) 'Self-development: Practical Issues for Group Facilitators', *Journal of European Industrial Training*, 13(5). A most helpful guide to setting up and facilitating self-development groups for people in organizations.

E4   Education for all

Provision on demand of widespread, not necessarily work-related education opportunities through and often at the workplace.

Pedler, M. J. *et al.* (1990) *Self-Development in Organisations*, McGraw-Hill, Maidenhead, UK. A book of case studies showing how self-development has been applied in mainly large organizational settings.

Wiggenhorn, W. (1990) 'Motorola U: When Training becomes an Education', *Harvard Business Review*, July/August, pp. 71–83. A readable account of Motorola's ambitious scheme to extend education and training to all employees worldwide *and* to employees of customers, suppliers and educational partners.

Williams, M. (1990) 'Learning to win', *Transition*, June, pp. 8–10. Case study of Rover Group's learning-for-all-approach.

Houghan, J., J. Thomas and K. Sisson (1991) 'Ford's EDAP Scheme: a round table discussion', *Human Resource Management Journal*, 1(3), Spring, pp. 77–91. Usefully gives the trade union (MSF) view as well as management's.

F Spiritual development

Providing learning that takes account of the spiritual dimension—can sometimes be related to explicit company-wide statements about the place of the spirit in the organization.

Huxley, A. (1974) *The Perennial Philosophy*, Chatto & Windus, London. An erudite review of self-knowledge, God, truth, etc., drawn from most of the world's spiritual gurus. Wonderful.

Wilbur, K. (1980) *The ATMAN Project*, Theosophical Publishing House, Wheaton, Ill. A transpersonal view of human development—the age-old quest for oneness with God through a modern fusion of Eastern and Western psychology.

Steiner, R. (1970) *Theosophy*, Rudolf Steiner Press, London. Steiner's primer of 'supersensible' knowledge and how to come to full consciousness of self and world.

F1 Moral management
An approach to managing based on principles or doctrines from one of the world religions or codes of ethics.

Snell, R. (1990) 'Managers' development of ethical awareness and personal morality', *Personnel Review*, 19(1), pp. 13–19. Uses a stage model of ethical development, asks what challenges development, and explores an agenda for further research.

F2 Meditational approaches
Several traditions, of which perhaps the best known is transcendental meditation (TM), have been developed for use in a specifically organizational context.

Messing, B. (1989) *The Tao of Management*, Wildwood House, Aldershot. A lovely book by a practising CEO offering short koans to reflect upon.

F3 Corporate responsibility
An approach integrating F1 with making a case for the business effectiveness of this position.

Sawyer, G. (1979) *Business and Society: Managing Corporate Social Impact*, Houghton Mifflin, London. Business-centred but sensible review of the firm's responsibilities to its stakeholders.

F4.1 Values/business ethics
Building on F3, and emphasizing the process of clarifying existing values at individual and corporate levels, and then making conscious decisions about whether to change them and if so, how.

Morris, J. (1987) 'Good Company', *Management Education and Development*, 19(2), Summer, pp. 103–15. Seminal paper suggesting that companies must manage to the 'mutual advantage' of an ever-widening circle of stakeholders.

Large, Martin (1981) *Social Ecology.* Self-published at 25 Reservoir Road, Gloucester. A before-its-time analysis of post-industrial society linking human development with organizational and societal development.

Maclagan, P. (1991) 'From moral ideals to moral action: Lessons for Management Development', *Management Education and Development*, 22(1), Spring, pp. 3–14. A useful action-oriented analysis, with an emphasis on learning applications.

Fullerton, H. and C. Price (1991) 'Culture change in the NHS', *Personnel Management*, 23(3), March, pp. 50–4. Reports on Grampian Health Board overhauling their value system since 1986. Describes shifts on eight themes by seven staff groups at four levels.

F4.2 Green organization
Exploring the effect of making decisions in the organization that take into account environmental considerations. Facilitating action on these decisions.

Hutchinson, C. (1991) *Business and the Environmental Challenge: A Guide for Managers*, The Conservation Trust, Reading, Berks. Spells out the issues very clearly with charts and diagrams. Looks at what companies are doing, and offers a checklist for an environmental programme.

Adams, R., J. Carruthers and S. Hamil (1991) *Changing Corporate Values*, Kogan Page/New Consumer, Newcastle upon Tyne. Surveys 128 UK consumer companies in terms of 13 environmental and other dimensions.

Davis, J. (1991) *Greening Business—Managing for Sustainable Development*, Blackwell, Oxford. An engineer writing in a soft-edged field, offering codes of practice for sustainable global development.

F4.3 Spirituality in organizations
Integrating spiritual issues into organization decisions, and using the spiritual dimension specifically to inform organizational processes. The best known approach may be Rudolf Steiner's anthroposophy.

Harrison, R. (1983) 'Strategies for a New Age', *Human Resources Management*, 22(3), pp. 209–35. Holistic view that asks what our organizations are for and suggests that strategic thinking should be a search for meaning rather than for narrow advantage. From this global viewpoint, companies belong to the planet and only those that fit will serve.

Owen, H. (1987) *Spirit, Transformation and Development in Organisations*, Abbott Publishing, Potomac, MD. Spiritual knowledge is needed to transform rather than (incrementally) develop people and organizations. A powerful, and personal, introduction to organization transformation ideas.

G Physical approaches

Using physical activity or artistic expression to confront developmental issues in a way that 'talking about' things often does not address.

G1 Muscular Christianity

Using the notion of *mens sana in corpore sano* (healthy mind: healthy body) as a basis for toughening up managers and increasing their self-confidence.

Baden-Powell, R. (1953) *Scouting for Boys* (27th ed.), CA Pearson, London. From the man who never started a day without some vigorous physical exercise and who influenced a lot of us.

G2 Outward Bound

Using challenging outdoor experiences (e.g. canoeing, climbing, abseiling) as a means of encouraging self-confrontation and development.

Beeby, M. and S. Rathborn (1983) 'Development Training: Using the Outdoors for Management Development', *Management Education and Development*, 14(3), Winter, pp. 170–81. Defines nature and scope of outdoor management development and examines why so many trainers remain distrustful.

G3.1 Outdoor development

Balancing challenge in the outdoors with an emphasis on decision making and group work. Highlighting the fact that physical strength or stamina are not the touchstones of excellence, but what you do with what you've got.

Radcliff, P. and P. Keslake (1981) 'Outward Bound?' in Boydell, T. and M. Pedler (eds), *Management Self-development Concepts and Applications*, Gower, 1981, pp. 85–98. Suggests that a physical environment may stimulate personal risk, exposure and self-examination. Outward Bound and Inward Bound are linked.

Mossmann, A. (1983) 'Making Choices: Using the Outdoors in Management Development', *Management Education and Development*, 14(3), Winter, pp. 182–96. Useful analysis of outdoor management development from several perspectives—adventure education, manager training, self-development and diagnosis. Contains a good bibliography.

G3.2 Artistic expression

Using dance (eurhythmy), painting, clay modelling, poetry writing, etc., to counterbalance predominantly left-brain styles of managing and learning.

Ernst, S. and L. Goodison (1981) *In our own Hands: A Book of Self-help Therapy*, Women's Press, London. Frameworks and exercises from a women's self-help point of view (and useful for many other groups too)—see especially Chapter 5 and 7.

G4 Total well-being

An approach that combines health monitoring, exercise programmes and stress management (see C4.2).

Pedler, M. and T. Boydell (1990) *Managing Yourself*, Gower, Aldershot. Especially Chapter 6, 'Managing your health'.

H Equal opportunities

Many developers took up an aspect of equal opportunities—usually race or gender—and added this to other approaches. In a contrary direction, specialists in an aspect of equal opportunities have often become developers taking on other areas and techniques.

H1 Cultural assimilation

Early workers in this field were concerned to help immigrants to Britain learn local *mores* and styles of managing. In some cases English language tuition was also provided.

Vize, R. (1990) 'Rarely fair', *Personnel Today*, 9 October, pp. 35–6. Outlines the application of the Fair Employment Act (Northern Ireland), and explores the extent to which this might prove a legislative way forward for equal opportunities in the UK.

H2 Racism/sexism awareness training

The emphasis shifted to training the potential oppressors in awareness of the impact of their individual actions and of institutionalized discrimination.

Davidson, M. J. and J. Earnshaw (1990) 'Policies, practices, and attitudes towards sexual harassment in UK organisations', *Personnel Review*, 19(3), pp. 23–7. Thorough research into the attitudes and equal opportunity practices of personnel directors.

H3 Women's/men's development and multiculturalism

Development focusing on the particular contribution of men/women and of white/black cultures, and recognizing, valuing and using the strengths of each.

Mogood, T. (1990) 'Colour, class and culture: the three Cs of race', *Equal Opportunities Review*, No. 30, March/April, pp. 31–3. A thoughtful article highlighting cultural insensitivities in recruitment and selection, and calling for improved training and learning materials.

Coyle, A. and J. Skinner (1988) *Women and Work: Positive Action for Change*, Macmillan, Basingstoke. Combining case studies and conceptual analyses; final chapter by Rennie Fritchie emphasizes place of training.

Online Productions (1985) *It Worked Fine: Managing Disabled Employees*, Manpower Services Commission, Sheffield. A useful video, with supporting booklet, showing examples of good practice in private and public sectors.

H4 Flexible firm/HRD strategy

Development directed to ensuring that all employees receive appropriate training and development, so that none is disadvantaged.

Clutterbuck, D. and D. Snow (1990) *Working with the Community: A Guide to Corporate Social Responsibility*, Weidenfeld & Nicolson, London.

Chapter 2 'Responsibilities towards employees' is a broad summary including equal opportunity requirements within the wider framework of responsibility.

Prowse, P. (1990) 'Assessing the flexible firm', *Personnel Review*, 19(6), pp. 13–17. A useful review article.

I Focal group

Another way in which developers structure their work is by focusing on a particular level of management. In the different eras the fashionable group has switched around somewhat.

I1 Supervisors

In the early days it was supervisors who were trained, often through programmes that were highly general in nature and contained a large element of socialization and background information, rather than specific skill development.

Walton, R. (1985) 'From control to commitment in the workplace', *Harvard Business Review*, March/April. A new look at the role of the supervisor.

I2 Graduates

The emphasis shifted to graduates, though the training approach remained much the same; with graduates, however, some attention was given to experience at work and job rotation.

Leibowitz, Z. B., N. K. Schlossberg and J. E. Shore (1991) 'Stopping the revolving door', *Training and Development Journal*, 45(2), February, pp. 43–56. A practical, helpful, model-rich article.

Schofield, P. (1991) 'The difference a graduate recruitment brochure can make', *Personnel Management*, 23(1), January, pp. 36–9. Examines what graduates are looking for at the recruitment phase.

I3 Middle managers

Supervisors frequently said, 'It's our bosses you should have on these courses', so developers obliged. Case studies and role plays were widely used. Leadership was often a focus.

Edwards, P. K. (1987) *Managing the Factory*, Blackwell, Oxford. A survey of over 200 factory managers, highlighting the informality and patchiness of their development.

I4 Everyone a manager

Recently some developers have changed the focus to giving training to all staff in how to think and act managerially. This approach often links with the Excellence approach (see K3) and with Total Quality Management (see M4).

Kelley, R. E. (1988) 'In praise of followers', *Harvard Business Review*, 66(6), Nov/Dec, pp. 142–8. Effective followers manage themselves well, are committed to the organization, build their competence and are courageous, honest and credible—in short, they're leaders.

Group streams

J Group training
Many developers found that focusing on individual development omitted certain key factors. It was only when the core focus was the group itself that learning about interaction could be fully grasped.

J1 T-groups
Parallel with the Tavistock groups (see C1) in Britain, T-groups were developed at national training laboratories in the USA. They involved the facilitator creating a leadership vacuum, and then offering process comments to help participants recognize their response to this. Facilitators offered their own feelings in the situation, and were less remote than in the Tavistock model.

Conyne, R. K. (1989) *How Personal Growth and Task Groups Work*, Sage, Newbury Park, Ca. Studies just two groups in intensive detail, with theoretical underpinning and helpful annotated bibliography.

J2.1 Encounter
One development from the T-group was the encounter group, where the predominantly unstructured group was enriched by the trainer introducing from time to time experiential exercises, designed to high-light the processes that the facilitator saw taking place in the group.

Schutz, W. (1968) *Joy*, Penguin, Harmondsworth. A delightful classic in this area.

J2.2 Structured experiences
Uses the experiential method of the previous two types, but removes the ambiguity about the direction the group should take by having the trainer decide, often according to a predetermined programme, which exercise should be done and when.

Pfeiffer, J. W. (1990) *The Annual: Developing Human Resources*, University Associates, San Diego, Ca. Part of a 20-year-long sequence of activities, lecturettes and instruments that has flowed from this taming of the raw power of the unstructured group.

J3 Team building
Uses the learning technology developed in the above approaches, but with intact work teams. An attempt to overcome the problem of transfer of training back to the workplace. Nowadays often referred to as 'awaydays', and having less emphasis on structured experiences, and making more use of 'Excellence' ideas (see K3).

Larson, C. E. and M. J. LaFasto (1989) *Teamwork: What must go Right/ What can go Wrong*, Sage, Newbury Park, Ca. An intriguing analysis of a diverse collection of teams, helpfully conceptualized.

Woodcock, M. (1989) *Team Development Manual* (2nd ed.), Gower, Aldershot. A comprehensive how-to manual.

Handy, C. (1990) *Handy on Teams*, BBC Training Videos, London. Examines key factors in developing teams, emphasizing the importance of a clear vision.

J4   Networking/cross-functional working
A response to the recognition that building strong teams can also build strong barriers between them. Developers using this perspective work with groups representing a wide range of interests in the organization and, indeed, those outside the organization (customers, suppliers, neighbours) to build effective working relationships and systems.

Lessem, R. (1989) *Global Management Principles*, Prentice-Hall, Hemel Hempstead. Section D of this monumental tome explores the importance and use of networks.

Organization streams

K   Organizational
Some developers emphasized that it was only by focusing on the whole organization and using social science insights that development that would have a lasting impact and be able to address the deeper needs of the organization.

K1   Survey feedback
By exploring the views of staff or customers in a systematic manner, decision makers identified areas for improvement, and acted upon them.

Likert, R. (1961) *New Patterns of Management*, McGraw-Hill, NY. See particularly Chapter 5—the effect of measuring on management practices.

K2   Organization development
A long-range effort to improve the organization's problem-solving and renewal processes through collaborative diagnosis and management of organizational culture, using applied behavioural science theory and technology (French and Bell 1984).

Plant, R. (1987) *Managing Change and Making it Stick*, Fontana, London. A helpful, model-rich, how-to book.

Carnall, C. (1990) *Managing Change in Organisations*, Prentice-Hall, Hemel Hempstead. A rigorous, well-referenced text, with some practical focus as well.

Handy, C. (1990) *Handy on Teams*, BBC Training Videos, London. Compares successful and unsuccesssful examples of change management and draws lessons from the differences.

French, W. L. and C. H. Bell (1984) *Organization Development*, Prentice-Hall, NJ. A structures introduction to the field.

K3   Excellence
Modelling change processes on the best practice in other organizations that are responding effectively to the increasingly global challenges faced by all organizations.

Peters, T. (1987) *Thriving on Chaos*, Macmillan, London. Love him or hate him, he's hard to ignore. At least with the book you don't see Peters spitting on the front three rows of the audience. A seminal and challenging text.

Lessem, R. (1985) *The Roots of Excellence*, Fontana, London. Tries to get below the gloss of Peters. His examples have a dated feel, including Sinclair Research and ICI.

Heckler, L. (1990) *Achieving Excellence*, Career Track International, Milton Keynes. A 4-sided audio tape, with helpful how-to advice.

K4.1   Organization transformation
An integration of the above approaches, recognizing that such change cannot be piecemeal, but requires a radical, long-term effort that transforms power relations and culture in a comprehensive way.

Torbert, W. (1991) *The Power of Balance: Transforming Self, Society and Scientific Enquiry*, Sage, Newbury Park, Ca. A demanding read, but rewarding in its insights into both the creation of liberating structures and the methods of action enquiry.

Owen, H. (1987) *Spirit, Transformation and Development in Organizations*, Abbott, Potomac, MD. Emphasizes the place of the spirit in transforming organizations.

K4.2   Learning Company
Creating a company that facilitates the learning of all its members *and* continuously transforms itself (Pedler, Boydell and Burgoyne 1988).

Pedler, M. J., J. E. Burgoyne and T. H. Boydell (1991) *The Learning Company: A Strategy for Sustainable Development*, McGraw-Hill, Maidenhead. A practical vision of how to create self-development opportunities for all organization members while transforming the whole.

Garratt, B. (1987) *The Learning Organisation: and the Need for Directors who think*, Fontana, London. As the title suggests, this book focuses on the role of directors, and provides some useful models of the links between policy, strategy formation and operations.

L   Strategy development
Corporate planners have recognized that if they want their plans implemented then they must get into the development business.

L1   Policy making
Creating a direction for the organization by the development of written statements of intended procedures and outcomes for areas of organizational life.

Ansoff, I. (1987) *Corporate Strategy*, Penguin, Harmondsworth. Chapter 6 explains the link between policy and the wider and more recent concept of strategy.

L2   Management by objectives (MBO)
A process by which the organizational need for planning is linked into

the individual manager's need to specify the outputs of the job and to have the freedom to determine the means whereby these outputs will be achieved.

Fowler, A. (1990) 'Performance management: the MBO of the '90s?' *Personnel Management*, 22(7), July, pp. 47–51. Compares performance management and MBO, and emphasizes the need for personnel managers to be the integrators and developers of the ideas, rather than the owners.

L3   Business planning
As well as individual policies and managers' targets, organizations also need an overall planning framework that includes financial plans.

Chandler, J. (1987) *Practical Business Planning*, McGraw-Hill, Maidenhead. What it is and how to manage it.

L4   Strategy formation
The process of forming strategy can go beyond extrapolating trends, and can involve a reappraisal of the direction of the enterprise and its constituent parts.

Quinn, J. B., H. Mintzberg and R. M. James (1988) *The Strategy Process: Concepts, Contexts and Cases*, Prentice-Hall, Englewood Cliffs, NJ. A blockbuster, strengthened by being based on Mintzberg's strong model of organizational types.

Kanter, R. M. (1990) *When Giants Learn to Dance*, Unwin, London. Sometimes described as the thinking person's Tom Peters, she reviews the changes large organizations are having to make in the 90s.

Cooke, R. and M. Armstrong (1990) 'The search for strategic HRM', *Personnel Management*, December, 22(12), pp. 30–3. A basic introduction to strategy and HRM's part in it.

M   Quality
A concern for the quality of the organization's output can lead to a recognition of the need for development. This link has grown much stronger in recent years.

M1   Inspection
Examining intermediate and finished goods to ascertain whether they conform to specification, and arranging for re-work or scrapping in the event of non-conformity.

M2   Quality control
Building in a departmental responsibility for quality, so that quality considerations are fed into the process of management decision making.

M3   Quality assurance
Recognizing that quality will only be attained by ensuring that all organizational systems are designed to contribute to setting and maintaining a standard. BS5750 and ISO9000 are examples of quality assurance systems.

Giles, E. (1991) 'Can the personnel department survive quality management?' *Personnel Management*, 23(4), April, pp. 28–33. Outlines BS5750 and looks towards what lies beyond this quality assurance approach.

M4 Total quality management (TQM)
Using statistical methods to determine conformity, and using the efforts of all employees and other stakeholders to determine directions for continuous improvement.

Crosby, P. (1989) *Crosby on Quality*, BBC Training Videos, London. A double video. In the first, you get Crosby's certainties around his four absolutes of quality; in the second there are some interesting case studies.

Deming, W. E. (1988) *Out of the Crisis*, Cambridge University Press, Cambridge. Deming's more thoughtful and deeper approach contrasts with Crosby's.

N Ownership
This strand of development aims at improvement through changing structures of power or ownership between the various stakeholders in the organization.

N1 Welfarism
Emphasizes the right of workers to a fair reward for their efforts, good conditions in which to carry out their work and justice in their relations with the organization.

Reynolds, B. (1989) *The 100 Best Companies to Work for in the UK*, Fontana, London. An interesting twist to the welfare saga—graduates are advised to work for organizations that look after them.

N2 Co-operatives/autonomous work groups
Fundamental changes in ownership or the role of management can lead to an opportunity for all workers to make a full contribution to the enterprise, and to reap the full rewards.

Davis, J. (1991) *Greening Business: Managing for sustainable Development*, Blackwell, Oxford. Chapter 7 'Pulling together—alternative ownership' provides a current summary of some radical ownership initiatives and a thoughtful analysis of the principles that might inform different ownership relations.

N3 Wider share ownership
The notion that large organizations can be changed by enabling the workforce to become shareholders as well, so that the conflict of interests between workforce and owners is minimized.

Carrington, L. (1991) 'Measure Success', *Personnel Today*, 14 May, pp. 27–8. A useful summary of profit sharing, Esops and Save as you Earn.

N4 Stakeholder relations
If customers and suppliers (and indeed neighbours and competitors) are

seen as having a stake in the organization, then developers can help to create new, collaborative relations between the parties.

Clutterbuck, D. and D. Shaw (1991) *Working with the Community: A Guide to Corporate Social Responsibility*, Weidenfeld & Nicolson, London. Based on a survey, full of case studies and checklists, and covering customers, employees, suppliers, shareholders, the political arena, the community and the environment.

Carlisle, J. A. and R. C. Parker (1989) *Beyond Negotiation: Redeeming Customer–Supplier Relationships*, Wiley, Chichester. A wise book, that could also be a source for total quality management and for ethical management. An example of how these fields seem to be converging.

O   Technology

The relationship between people and their technology has profound implications for development, reaching far beyond the mere need for technical training.

O1   Mechanization
The mechanization of, first, factory work and then office work had a profound effect on development. Work study and organization and methods specialists increasingly determined and specified the exact nature of jobs, which were often tightly circumscribed.

O2   Group technology
The negative motivational effects of mechanization were compensated for by enriching jobs and organizing significant tasks to be performed by groups of workers who had some responsibility for planning their own time.

Rosow, J. M. and R. Zager (1988) *Training—The Competitive Edge*, Jossey-Bass, San Francisco, Ca. Three-year study on how companies can best work with the new technologies.

O3   Automation
Transferring the 'doing' tasks from people to machines led to changes in work relations between managers and managed, as well as the need for new skills for the new knowledge workers.

Goodman, A. and M. W. Lawless (1988) *Technology and Strategy*, Addison-Wesley, Englewood Cliffs, NJ. Linking developments in automation to other strategic issues.

O4   Integrated manufacture
The divisions between design, planning, manufacture and quality start to blur, with important implications for the organization of work and the relationship between different functions.

Schonberger, R. J. (1986) *World Class Manufacturing*, Free Press, NY. This book draws together much that has gone before and presents a formidable challenge to those of us tempted to keep our heads in the sand of soft development, and to remain as big fishes in a small organizational pond.

Afterword

The last review—of Schonberger's book—represents a conclusion of a kind. A lot of strands of development seem to be coming together. But perhaps the past always seems like that when viewed from the present. However much convergence there really is, it seems clear to us that plenty of diversity will remain for developers to pick their own unique way. This book is dedicated to this process of choosing a unique path and to the connections that we will make on the way.

Bibliography

Argyle, M. (1989) *The Social Psychology of Work* (2nd ed.) Penguin, Harmondsworth.

Argyris, C. and D. A. Schon (1978) *Organisational Learning: A Theory in Action Perspective*, Addison-Wesley, Reading, Mass.

Bateson, G. (1986) *Steps to an Ecology of Mind*, Paladin, London.

Belbin, E. and R. M. (1972) *Problems in Adult Retraining*, Heinemann, London.

Brown, W. (1971) *Organisation*, Heinemann, London.

Burns, T. and N. Stalker (1959) *The Management of Innovation*, Tavistock, London.

Carlisle, J. and R. Parker (1990) *Beyond Negotiation: Redeeming Customer–Supplier Relationships*, McGraw-Hill, Maidenhead.

Carnegie, D. (1953) *How to Win Friends and Influence People*, Worlds Work, Kingsworth.

Chandler, A. (1962) *Strategy and Structure*, Doubleday, NY.

Clutterbuck, D. (1991) *Everyone needs a Mentor* (2nd ed.), Institute of Personnel Management, London.

Daloz, L. A. (1986) *Effective Teaching and Mentoring*, Jossey-Bass, San Francisco.

Davis, J. (1991) *Greening Business: Managing for Sustainable Development*, Blackwell, Oxford.

Deming, W. E. (1988) *Out of the Crisis*, Cambridge University Press, Cambridge.

Fowler, A. (1990) 'Performance management: the MBO of the '90s?' *Personnel Management*, 22(7), pp. 47–51.

Gergen, K. (1978) 'Towards Generative Theory', *Journal of Personality and Social Psychology*, 36, pp. 1344–60.

Hamel, G. and C. K. Prahalad (1989) 'Strategic Intent', *Harvard Business Review*, May–June, pp. 63–76.

Harris, T. (1973) *I'm OK: You're OK*, Pan, London.

Harrison, R. (1987) *Organisation Culture and Quality of Service: a strategy for releasing love in the workplace*, AMED, London.

Jackins, H. (1973) *The human situation*, Rational Island, Seattle.

Kemp, N. (1989) 'Self-development: practical issues for facilitators', *Journal of European Industrial Training*, 13(5), pp. 1–28.

Knevitt, C. (1985) *Space on earth*, Thames TV International, London.

Kolb, D. (1985) *Experiential Learning*, Prentice-Hall, NY.

Larson, C. E. and M. J. LaFasto (1989) *Teamwork: what must go right/what can go wrong*, Sage, Newbury Park, Ca.

Leary, J. and M. Leary 'Transforming your career', Chapter 10 in Pedler, Burgoyne and Boydell (1988).

Lessem, R. (1989) *Global Management Principles*, Prentice-Hall, Hemel Hempstead.

McCaskey, M. (1988) 'The Challenge of Managing Ambiguity and Change', in Pondy, Boland and Thomas (eds), *Managing Ambiguity and Change*, Wiley, Chichester, pp. 1–15.

McConnell, D. and V. Hodgson (1990) 'Computer Mediated Communications Systems (CMCS)—Electronic Networking and Education', *Management Education & Development*, 21(1), Spring, pp. 51–8.

Megginson, D. and T. Boydell (1979) *A Manager's Guide to Coaching*, BACIE, London.

Mintzberg, H. (1979) *The Structure of Organizations*, Prentice-Hall, Englewood Cliffs, NJ.

Mumford, A. 'Learning to learn and management self-development', Chapter 2 in Pedler, Burgoyne and Boydell (1988).

Pedler, M. J. (1986) 'Development within the organisation: experiences with management self-development groups', *Management and Education Development*, 17(1), pp. 5–21.

Pedler, M. J. (ed.) (1991) *Action Learning in Practice* (2nd ed.), Gower Press, Aldershot.

Pedler, M. J. and T. H. Boydell (1985) *Managing Yourself*, Fontana, London.

Pedler, M. J., T. H. Boydell and J. G. Burgoyne (1988) 'Learning Company Project Report', *Training Agency*, Sheffield.

Pedler, M. J., T. H. Boydell and J. G. Burgoyne (1989) 'Towards the Learning Company', *Management Education & Development*, 20(1), pp. 1–8.

Pedler, M. J., J. G. Burgoyne and T. H. Boydell (1986) *A Manager's Guide to Self-development* (2nd ed.) McGraw-Hill, Maidenhead.

Pedler, M. J., J. G. Burgoyne and T. H. Boydell (1988) *Applying Self-development in Organizations*, Prentice-Hall, Hemel Hempstead.

Pedler, M. J., J. G. Burgoyne and T. H. Boydell (1991) *The Learning Company: A Strategy for Sustainable Development*, McGraw-Hill, Maidenhead.

Peters, T. (1987) *Thriving on Chaos*, Macmillan, London.

Peters, T. J. and R. H. Waterman, Jr. (1982) *In Search of Excellence: Lessons from America's Best-Run Companies*, Harper and Row, NY.

Porter, M. (1982) *Competitive Strategy*, Macmillan, NY.

Revans, R. W. (1982) *The Origins and Growth of Action Learning*, Chartwell-Bratt, Bromley.

Revans, R. W. (1983) *The ABC of Action Learning*, Chartwell-Bratt, Bromley.

Smiles, S. (1859) *Self Help*, Murray, London.

Ward, J. N. (1986) *Friday Afternoon*, Epworth, London.

Woodcock, M. (1989) *Team Development Manual* (2nd ed.), Gower, Aldershot.

Name index

Subject index